Language Knowledge for Primary Teachers

Teaching children to develop as language users is one of the most important tasks of a primary school teacher. However, many trainee teachers begin their career with a low knowledge base.

Language Knowledge for Primary Teachers is the reader-friendly guide designed to address this. This book provides a clear explanation of the knowledge and understanding required by teachers to implement the objectives of the National Curriculum for English. It reveals how an explicit knowledge of language can enrich their own and their children's spoken English. It will give teachers confidence in developing children's enjoyment and comprehension of reading and writing so that children can use their language skills in the real world.

Updated to include references to the new curriculum, this book explores:

- the importance of subject knowledge in supporting children in language and literacy;
- language knowledge within the context of authentic and meaningful texts, from fiction to Facebook;
- the links between subject knowledge and real teaching situations;
- new areas on talk and dialogic learning;
- the increased emphasis on Information and Communication Technologies (ICT) and cross-curricular study.

This book will appeal to all trainee and newly qualified teachers needing both to meet the demands of subject knowledge for Qualified Teacher Status and acquire a firm understanding of the expectations of the National Curriculum for English.

Angela Wilson is former Senior Lecturer in Education at the North East Wales Institute of Higher Education, now Glyndŵr University.

Julie Scanlon is Senior Lecturer in Primary English at Manchester Metropolitan University.

Language Knowledge for Primary Teachers

Fourth edition

By Angela Wilson and Julie Scanlon

Routledge
Taylor & Francis Group

LONDON AND NEW YORK

First edition published 1999
by David Fulton
Second edition published 2001
Third edition published 2005
This edition published 2011
by Routledge
2 Park Square, Milton Park, Abingdon, Oxon, OX14 4RN

Simultaneously published in the USA and Canada
by Routledge
270 Madison Avenue, New York, NY 10016

Routledge is an imprint of the Taylor & Francis Group, an informa business

© 2011 Angela Wilson and Julie Scanlon

Typeset in Bembo by Prepress Projects Ltd, UK
Printed and bound in Great Britain by TJ International Ltd, Padstow, Cornwall

British Library Cataloguing in Publication Data
A catalogue record for this book is available from the British Library

Library of Congress Cataloging-in-Publication Data
Wilson, Angela.
Language knowledge for primary teachers / by Angela Wilson and Julie Scanlon.–4th ed.
p. cm.
Includes bibliographical references and index.
1. English language–Study and teaching (Elementary)–Great Britain. I. Scanlon, Julie.
II. Title.
LB1576.W48875 2011
372.6'0440941–dc22
2010035108

ISBN13: 978-0-415-56481-6 (hbk)
ISBN13: 978-0-415-56480-9 (pbk)
ISBN13: 978-0-203-83100-7 (ebk)

For Andrew and for Isobel
For Andrew and for Jeremy

Contents

Illustrations

Figures

Acknowledgements

We are very grateful to all the children, students, colleagues and friends who have contributed in various ways to the production of this book. We would especially like to thank our families.

We would also like to thank the publishers, authors and colleagues who have been kind enough to grant permission for material to be reprinted, in particular D.C. Thomson Ltd for an extract from *The Beano*; John Byrne for the drawing from *Create Your Own Cartoons;* Hodder Arnold for an extract from *Living Language: Exploring Advanced Level English Language* by Keith and Shuttleworth; Multilingual Matters Ltd for 'My Language is my Home' by Pirkko Leporanta-Morley, quoted in *Minority Education* by Skutnabb-Kangas and Cummins; Kit Wright for '*The Frozen Man*'; and Mind Candy Ltd © for the Moshi Monsters web page, www.moshimonsters.com.

Introduction

Is this book for you?

In writing this book we had two audiences in mind. The first group is student teachers. The second includes all those primary teachers and teaching assistants who are trying to implement multi-strategy approaches to literacy, especially those who have felt challenged by the levels of language knowledge expected of them in recent government documents.

Government expectations

The government requires all entrants to teaching, at whatever phase, to have a secure knowledge and understanding of their subjects/curriculum areas (TDA 2006: 11). For language teaching at the Foundation Stage (three to five year olds) the requirement is to know and understand the aims, principles and relevant areas of learning set out under the heading of 'Communication, Language and Literacy' in the Early Learning Goals (DCSF 2008), which describe what most children should achieve by the end of their reception year. For Key Stage 1 (five to seven year olds) and Key Stage 2 (seven to 11 year olds) teachers must know and understand the National Curriculum for English (DfEE/QCA 1999).

Whichever government strategy is in place, and they seem to come and go with bewildering speed, nothing at all worthwhile will have been achieved if we cannot help children to enjoy using and encountering language in all its forms. And language not only brings enjoyment, it is massively empowering too. Teachers can best bring this joy and power to children if they themselves are confident and knowledgeable about language, a view supported by Earl *et al.* (2003).

We presume that you have picked up this book because you are training to be a primary teacher or are already teaching in the Early Years Foundation Stage or Key Stages 1 or 2. In our view, the question you need to keep in mind as you consider your language knowledge is 'Do I know enough to help me to enthuse and excite children to extend and develop their experience of language?' You may be tempted to answer 'No!', but if you decide to go on reading you're very likely to find that you know more than you think you do. Part of your negative response may come from a feeling that you don't have the right terminology in which to express your knowledge. Terminology can be useful, but it is not the most important aspect of language study (see Activity 1(d), 'Putting into words what we know about language').

The fact that you are teaching in the early stages of schooling does not mean that a very basic level of language knowledge will suffice. (See Chapter 1 of this book for some discussion of how much you need to know.) However, the uses you will make of your language knowledge are different from those that, say, an academic linguist would be concerned with. There are people whose life's work is the study of phonology or syntax, and there are others who will spend many a happy hour writing to the newspapers about a perceived abuse of a grammatical rule. Your position is different from both of these. Above all, your task is to help children to discover the wonder and excitement and power in making a text or in sharing one.

The difficult issues arise when you try to decide specifically what to do to foster this excitement. It's a question not just of what you as a teacher come to know about language, but of how skilful you are in interacting with the children you teach. What kinds of 'knowing about language' will increase the children's language powers, which are already impressive even before they come to school? Are there some kinds of language teaching that might even get in the way of the children's development? You might like to spend a few minutes on Activity 1 to get you started on thinking about some of the important aspects of language teaching in the primary context. A commentary on the activity is on page 162.

Activity 1: Setting the primary teaching context

Try making a few notes under four broad headings:

(a) Home/school contrasts

What would you say are the similarities and contrasts between the kinds of language a child uses at home and the language demands of school? (Think about the purposes of talk, who does the talking, and what they know about each other.)

(b) Speech/writing contrasts

Think about some of the speaking – and writing – you have done in the last few days. What similarities and contrasts can you think of between the spoken and the written language you used on these occasions?

(c) Language as a process and language as a product

What kinds of language skills and knowledge are you as an adult drawing on, probably without even thinking about it, that enabled you to do that speaking and writing? Which aspects of the speaking or writing were the most difficult for you? Why was that?

(d) Putting into words what we know about language

How could you turn what you know implicitly about language into explicit knowledge so that you could share it with children? Similarly, what would you need to do to help them to share what they know implicitly, with you and with each other?

Why not take twenty minutes or so to consider these questions? See if you can jot down two or three points in response to each one. Don't worry if you can't manage as many points as that at this stage. You will find ideas to help you if you read the chapters of this book. You could try the activity again after you have read some of them, and we hope that then you will feel that you have developed your thinking.

My language is my home

In my mother tongue my
hatred is sanguineous,
my love soft.
My innermost soul
is in balance
with my language.
The closeness of it
caresses my hair.
It has grown
together with me,
has taken roots in me.
My language
can be painted over
but not detached
without tearing
the structure of my cells.
If you paint a foreign language
on my skin
my innermost soul
cannot breathe.
The glow of my feelings
will not get through
the blocked pores.
There will be
a burning fever
rising for a way
to express itself.

(Pirkko Leporanta-Morley, quoted in Skutnabb-Kangas and Cummins 1988)

The background to language knowledge

1

Why do primary teachers need language knowledge?

Those who teach children in the Early Years and in Key Stages 1 and 2 are meeting them at a most crucial stage in their language development. It is you, for example, who will help them to make important developments in their speaking and listening. So far, many children might only have participated in groups in which the adults understand the children so well that they know what they want to say almost before they have said anything at all. You can help them to use language to reach out to others and to increase the range of speech tasks they can accomplish. The *Independent Review of the Teaching of Early Reading* by Rose makes the following point:

> The indications are that far more attention needs to be given, right from the start, to promoting speaking and listening skills to make sure that children build a good stock of words, learn to listen attentively and speak clearly and confidently.
>
> (Rose 2006: 3)

Some fortunate children will come to you already enjoying songs, nursery rhymes and stories. Some will have little or no experience of these. For all of them, you can extend their enjoyment and help them to become independent readers. Crucially, this means helping them not only to learn how to read but also to know what reading has to offer them in all aspects of their lives. Some will already have the confidence to write, even if this means making marks on the paper to share what they want to say. Again, many will depend on you to start them off and to build up the range of purposes for writing that they can confidently tackle.

This is a daunting agenda and to be a creative, exciting and motivating teacher you need to feel confident about your own uses of language. We all acquire language knowledge as part of living our lives: we listen and we talk; we read and we write. Some of us do more of these things than others, and the kinds of speaking, listening, reading and writing we do will vary enormously. But what specific kinds of language knowledge do we need to be successful primary teachers?

Government requirements

One way of answering this question is to look at the documentation that has been published setting out what the government expects primary teachers to cover. There has been a lot of this over the last three decades. Some of it is still with us, some has been and gone and some may soon be on its way out. So not perhaps an ideal guide! However, a brief overview will introduce you to some of the topics in the documents that will remain important for you to consider, whatever the current legislation. References are given to where these topics receive further coverage throughout the book.

The Early Years Foundation Stage (DCSF 2008)

Extending the range

One very important concept has already been mentioned in the second paragraph of this chapter; purpose. The Early Years Foundation Stage (EYFS) curriculum encourages you to extend children's reading, writing and speaking for a range of purposes. If you have not thought about what this means before, just consider for a moment the kinds of reading, writing and talking you have done recently. Perhaps you have read a novel or searched for information about your holiday destination. You may have sympathised with a friend or explained to a plumber what has happened to your washing machine. As you move from task to task you quickly adjust your language according to what the situation requires. Sometimes this can be challenging. In speaking, and often in writing too, you take into account what you know about the other people involved: how long you have known them, how old they are, what their needs are etc. It would be a mistake to think that young children's spoken language is used by them only to meet their physical needs, though that is important. As well as telling us when they are hungry, thirsty, cold etc. they love to join in with what is happening around them, to share family jokes and stories, to remember a shared outing or plan a visit. The EYFS curriculum rightly encourages you to listen carefully to them. You may be very surprised at the 'meaning young children generate in their language through the creative ways in which they use words' (DCSF 2008: 42). But these children have a lot to learn. The range of purposes for speaking, let alone writing and reading, that the children encounter will inevitably be limited to the situations that their families or other caregivers introduce them to.

One big challenge for children in the Early Years of schooling is that they are now meeting people, adults and other children, who scarcely know them. So the EYFS curriculum makes clear that they need help with using language for building social relationships. The things they say and write must increasingly stand alone, without an adult there who can offer an interpretation. Increasing confidence in speaking and listening is a crucial starting point. This means taking part in one-to-one conversations and in small groups. As time goes on, it might even mean saying something to the whole class or even the school. Sometimes there will be adults in the group; sometimes the children must negotiate what they want to say without an adult. Children should have opportunities to initiate topics themselves and know that they will be followed up. They should be encouraged to ask questions and expect to be helped to find answers.

Language as system

Another important strand throughout the EYFS curriculum has to do with the way languages are organised. This organisation can be seen at a number of levels. Sounds build into words; words are combined according to the rules of grammar to make utterances or sentences; sentences build into texts. (Of course, this is a drastic oversimplification.) The 'building rules' we use will depend very much on the purposes we have in mind when we speak or write. Speakers and writers make different selections from the available 'language pot'. It would be a mistake to think that encouraging children to become confident talkers will necessarily turn them into fluent writers. But encouraging children to become confident speakers in the Early Years will build their belief in themselves as having something to say that those around them want to share. Alongside building this oral experience you can gradually show them how to use the written language system with its spelling and punctuation rules, which help to make ideas clear when they are written down.

Children who operate within more than one system

The EYFS curriculum reminds you that you will meet children who have more than one language or dialect at their disposal and who can switch from one to another sometimes within the same utterance. There are differences within and between cultures and speech communities in the range of spoken and written sounds and symbols they make use of. For example, the sound represented by 'll' in written Welsh (as in 'Llandudno') does not exist in English. Some of your children will expect a written text to flow from right to left across the page. Some may nod their heads when they mean 'no'. The classroom should be a place where all the languages the children have experience of are heard and seen – and maybe some others as well!

The National Curriculum (1999)

The National Curriculum is a statutory document and, at the time of writing, is under review. However aspects of the English curriculum will undoubtedly remain. The current programmes of study for speaking, listening, reading and writing have a lot more to say about extending the range of purposes, which we saw was a crucial part of the EYFS language development. For example, at Key Stage 1 we are told that pupils should be taught to vary their writing to suit the purpose and reader. They should be taught to write in a range of forms, incorporating some of the different characteristics of those forms. The range should include narratives, notes, lists, captions, records, messages and instructions (DfEE/QCA 1999: 48–9).

By the time we reach Key Stage 2, the list includes:

- play scripts;
- reports;
- explanations;
- opinions;
- reviews;

- commentaries.

(DfEE/QCA 1999: 58)

The programmes of study for speaking and listening, and for reading, make it equally clear that children must become skilled practitioners in these modes too. In reading, this includes being able to:

- respond to a range of texts, showing understanding of significant ideas, themes, events and characters;
- locate ideas and information in reading non-fiction texts.

To achieve level 4 in speaking and listening, pupils should be able to:

- talk and listen with confidence in an increasing range of contexts;
- adapt their talk according to its purpose;
- develop ideas thoughtfully;
- describe events;
- convey their opinions clearly;
- listen carefully;
- make contributions and ask questions that are responsive to others' ideas and views;
- use appropriately some of the features of standard English vocabulary and grammar.

Language as process; language as product

An important aspect of the programmes of study for English is that, taken as a whole, they expect teachers to help children develop their language knowledge in two ways. In this chapter we have already touched on what these are. The first is in becoming more confident language *users,* that is, people who enjoy reading and writing and speaking and listening, and do these things with confidence. Here are some of the specific requirements:

- help children to vary their writing to suit the purpose and the reader;
- help them to become responsive readers, exploring ideas, themes, events and characters in the texts they encounter;
- encourage them to become enthusiastic and confident talkers.

If you can get this right you will have a classroom in which children are using language to understand the world better, including the world of reading and the media, and are finding in language ways to explore their own feelings and attitudes towards what these worlds portray. In response to their thinking and feeling, these children will create a range of texts, both written and spoken, that will bring pleasure and delight to themselves, their teachers, their parents and others. The talking, reading and writing will flow out, across the whole curriculum and beyond it.

But this is not the whole story. Another aspect of the programmes of study makes it clear that at the same time you should gradually be making children more familiar with language as a system, or a series of systems, as we described earlier on page 5. Children are not reinventing the language wheel; they are inheriting ways of doing things with language that have evolved and are evolving constantly within the cultures and social groups that each child is a member of. Here are some of these requirements from the programmes of study:

- show children how to organise and present their writing in different ways;
- ensure that they incorporate into their writing *some characteristics of the various forms*;
- ensure that children are taught the grammatical constructions that are characteristic of spoken standard English and to apply this knowledge appropriately in a range of contexts.

We think that to bring all these contrasting elements of language work together successfully constitutes a huge challenge for primary teachers and requires teachers who are confident in their grasp of language systems. Most importantly the children need to learn about the systems of the language in such a way that their own uses of language are genuinely enriched and enhanced.

Learning about language and developing language knowledge is not like learning how to make a sponge cake. In that case, as soon as you've read about how to do it, or watched someone else, you set about making one. Language knowledge, on the other hand, can be stored in the mind in a number of ways. For example, a group of Year 6 children we worked with had thoroughly enjoyed discussing conjunctions. They'd found examples in the text they were reading and made a poster for the classroom wall. They could remember a lot of examples and they knew that the teacher wanted them to make use of them. However, a scrutiny of their English books revealed that few of them had in fact done so. Yet their written work was lively and interesting. Sadly, because many of them had been given as a target 'use more conjunctions', in the short term they seemed destined for a feeling of failure. If they had tried to drag conjunctions into their writing 'willy-nilly' the results would probably have been disastrous. Perhaps it's not surprising that the government's targets for success at level 4 have remained elusive, especially in the area of writing. We still need more sensitive understanding of what it means to acquire and use language knowledge, particularly in the area of developing children's writing.

The National Literacy Strategy (DfEE 1998)

The National Literacy Strategy (NLS) set out, in overwhelming detail, a progression of learning objectives at text, sentence and word level. It was daring, because it made enormous demands on children – and on teachers. And the exciting thing was that some teachers helped some children to meet those demands. Not for the first time, we found out how mistaken we can be about what children can do if we impose a glass ceiling on them. But the NLS was dangerously overcrowded, positioning children on a 'production line' rather than helping them to feel like genuine readers and writers – real 'processors of language' in other words. Many teachers found it very difficult to transform the long lists of learning objectives into exciting, creative teaching. The Primary National Strategy, which evolved from the NLS, would, it was hoped, give teachers more flexibility.

The Primary National Strategy – Framework for Literacy (DCSF 2005)

This is a document that is current at the time of writing but apparently is to be phased out in 2011. It was hoped that it would give greater coherence and continuity within and between stages of development. Much of the detail of the NLS has been slimmed down to create a clearer set of outcomes to support teachers and practitioners in planning for progression. Nevertheless, it still presents a challenging agenda – for teachers as well as for children. Twelve strands of learning have been identified, with learning objectives aligned to each of the twelve strands, for each year group from reception. The twelve strands are linked to the three areas of English set out in the National Curriculum. The important topics we have already identified in this chapter are spelt out in some detail. Here, for example, we have objectives relating to how children must be taught to apply their knowledge of the structures of written English in a broad range of writing tasks:

- make decisions about form and purpose, identify success criteria and use them to evaluate their writing (Year 3);
- experiment with different forms and styles to write their own stories (Year 5);
- select words and language drawing on their knowledge of literary features and formal and informal writing (Year 6).

It is not surprising that the document states that good literacy teaching requires teachers who have a good knowledge of the subject.

Teachers as skilled language practitioners

We feel absolutely certain that only by building on their own language knowledge can teachers hope to foster the skills and the enthusiasm for language, and confidence in engaging with it, that children need. This may seem a tall order. Many students who embark on courses of teacher training do not come to college with a subject strength in English. The time they have available for studying English is relatively limited. Reading, let alone writing, may not be a favourite leisure-time occupation. However, there is no need to despair.

Reading a wide variety of texts

As far as reading is concerned, being a skilled practitioner does not mean engaging with the canon of English literature (though there are those who might see this as desirable, and even enjoyable!). It does mean reading widely from a range of types of text, such as those suggested in the electronic framework supporting the Primary National Strategy.

You may need to make some adjustments to the way you read, because you must be prepared to see a writer as someone who has some skill in constructing a text, someone who has chosen a word or a sentence with great care for the impact it might have on the reader. This applies just as much in the case of those who write non-fiction and those who write primarily with children in mind. In fact, many writers whose works end up being enjoyed by children did not write primarily with them in mind. C.S. Lewis, for example, the author of the *Narnia* books, makes the point that it just happens that the things he liked writing were the things that children liked reading. Of course, writers can never be sure of the effect their words will have on the reader. People who read a lot have more and more reading experience to bring to bear each time they read, as well as a mass of other general life experiences. This means the text is, to some extent, created anew in the mind of every reader each time it is read, though it would be surprising if people who share a culture did not frequently find a large measure of agreement about their responses to a book.

You may be surprised and perhaps a little daunted by these comments on reading, especially if you embarked on becoming a teacher with the idea that reading was simply something to do with turning sounds into written symbols or vice versa. Of course, that is a vital part of the process. We will try to show the relationship between the various aspects of the reading process as we understand it in later chapters.

Creating spoken and written texts

Being a skilled practitioner also means having the confidence to have a go at creating texts yourself – for a variety of purposes and readers. It means pushing your speaking skills into what are possibly new areas for you, such as modelling for the children the role of a doctor's receptionist in the home corner, which has been transformed into a surgery for the week, or reading aloud with enough enthusiasm and skill to hold a class spellbound. These are just a couple of examples. Why are they so important? Because if you can successfully turn yourself into a confident practitioner then you have some hope of retaining a clear grasp of what language knowledge is for. Above all, language is for making and sharing meanings. Sometimes these meanings need to be available quickly and easily, as in a recipe or a railway timetable or giving someone directions. Sometimes it's interesting to have to tease out the meaning from a piece of text, as frequently happens when we are reading a poem or a story. It may be that the writer is playing a joke on us – having fun with meaning. This is hugely enjoyable for all concerned. On some occasions, readers and listeners know that they are being given a biased view of events. We have all offered one ourselves when it has suited our purposes.

It isn't just the content of the message, however, that is useful or enjoyable. Often the way in which the content is presented is just as important. We have all felt cross with ourselves when we have messed up the telling of a joke or a shaggy dog story, and the whole effect is lost. In reading poetry, it is often the sound of the words that moves us as much as the message contained in them. There may be no message at all when the writer is just having fun with sounds or with nonsense words. Or let us take a more down-to-earth example. Suppose we hope to impress an employer by the clarity of a report we have written, or persuade a bank manager to part with some cash. Certainly meanings need to come across clearly, but especially in these last two examples we need to choose the style of writing or speaking that we have seen described in the National Curriculum as standard English. These activities, which we are engaging in because we hope to profit from them, are a far cry from the fun of gossiping with friends and making them laugh as we turn the day's disasters into a funny story, perhaps drawing on a shared regional dialect. (You can read more about standard and non-standard English in Chapter 6.)

Confident practitioners are willing to engage in all these activities and more. They embark on them with enthusiasm, expecting to receive profit or pleasure from them. They may find some of them difficult, but they know where to go for help. They are not afraid of making mistakes, but know how to set about correcting them. Teachers, as much as, or perhaps more than, any other group in society, need to be confident practitioners because they must fire children with their confidence and their enthusiasm.

Becoming a reflective language teacher

One of the most dramatic changes that has been introduced into primary language work is that children should not be expected to be just 'language producers'; they should also be able to reflect explicitly on the language that others have used. As we have seen, this requirement has been carried over into the Primary National Strategy Framework. From very early on in the process of developing children's literacy, teachers must help children to move into a more reflective stance towards language, which they can do only if they themselves are reflective readers and writers and speakers. So teachers must be people who talk about what they are reading, and help children to do the same. They must respond sensitively to children's writing, sharing with the child their enthusiasm for the child's achievement and perhaps suggesting areas for further work. After a role play is over, they will take a class through what has been said, highlighting especially interesting sections and discussing places where things could have been done differently.

A language for talking about language

Language knowledge can be shared with children by means of a metalanguage – a language for talking about language. There is quite a lot of it in all the government documents we have mentioned so far, and it can seem alienating. Primary teachers nowadays need to know what a conjunction is, and a text type, an affix, a simile and a metaphor. Is it all really necessary? Any group of people who want to perfect their craft or hobby or interest – be it horse racing or photography or growing chrysanthemums – find themselves becoming more absorbed in the vocabulary of their subject. It helps them to become more precise, to talk more specifically about what they know or want to find out. In a sense, it helps them to see more clearly, to become more discriminating. If they join a club, those in the know seem at first frighteningly 'expert'. Yet their interest and enthusiasm usually overcome the newcomer's feelings of anxiety and inadequacy. If we see explicit language knowledge in this light, it is surely a good thing. A class who have, with their teacher's encouragement, learned to talk more precisely about what they or others are discussing, reading and writing are not going to be afraid of language, or of metalanguage, but will use it to build their knowledge and interest.

There is, of course, a social as well as a language aspect to what is going on at the photography lecture or the chrysanthemum society. Technical terms representing explicit knowledge of all kinds can be used to shore up the expert's sense of superiority, to slam the door in the face of slow learners or ones lacking in confidence. Then it becomes a bad thing. The challenge for tomorrow's teachers is to develop and to share language knowledge with their pupils in such a way that their explicit teaching informs and strengthens the children's practice and builds their confidence in themselves.

Language study as an end in itself

Presented by an enthusiastic and skilful teacher, language knowledge is also interesting in its own right, even though there may not always be an immediate practical application of it. Some work on word derivation, for example, can be an interesting activity for its own sake. Good teaching about the way words develop and change can help to engender an interest in vocabulary, and in the long run this will probably enrich a child's reading and writing and speaking. It might also help with some spelling difficulties.

Wray and Medwell (1998: 9) warn that learning is a situated process:

> Why is it that a child who spells ten words correctly in a spelling test is likely to spell several of them wrongly when writing a story a short while afterwards? The answer is simply that the learning of the spelling is so inextricably bound up with the context of the learning that it cannot easily be applied outside of this context.

Not easily, no, but it can be applied. The activities would be better presented the other way round. The child has a go at using a new word or words in writing a story, perhaps after meeting the words in a shared reading context and discussing their origins and meanings with the teacher. If the words are spelt wrongly, then the teacher can make links with the previous experience: 'Do you remember when we came across this word in shared reading? We said that it belongs to the —— family. They all come from a shared root, ——.' The words generated from the children's writing can then go on to be part of the spelling test. Teachers and children will share an increasing number and range of learning contexts as a school year progresses, and it is an important part of a teacher's job to help children to make links from one context to another.

Finding a new way forward

Recent government documents may have given the impression of turning the clock back, of demanding the kinds of language knowledge from teachers and from children that some schools have resolutely turned away from for 40 years or more. The effect on entrants to courses of teacher training was perhaps similar to that on the timid new member of the chrysanthemum society. Feelings of alienation, of fear even, could rise strongly to the surface. For someone in this state of mind, acquiring knowledge about parts of speech, syntactic patterns, text types and so on can all too easily become ends in themselves. We hope that in subsequent chapters of this book we can help student teachers to develop the language knowledge they need in order to become sensitive and confident teachers, so that language work both becomes an interesting study in its own right but, more importantly, helps us all to find further ways of developing children's reading, writing and speaking.

Summary

In this chapter we have discussed:

- recent government documentation relating to the teaching of English in primary schools;

- how language can be seen as a process, helping us to explore our experience and build our world view;

- how language can be seen as a product: a set of rules, expectations and ways of doing things that children are initiated into by members of their language communities;

- how teachers can equip themselves with language knowledge to support children in learning through language and learning about language.

2

A framework for considering language knowledge

In Chapter 1 we introduced the concepts of language as process and language as product or system. We urged you to see it as vitally important to your work as a primary teacher to increase your own confidence and skills in the processes of language. We hope we have said enough to convince you of how important this is and that you have already started to explore some writing for children that is new to you as well as writing something of your own!

In most of the subsequent chapters of this book we will be mainly concerned with aspects of the language system, though always in the context of exploring how knowing more about the system might help in becoming a more informed and reflective practitioner. In the arrangement of the chapters we have adopted a three-part framework:

■ What do primary teachers need to know about texts and how they are constructed?

■ What should they know about the rules of syntax and punctuation?

■ What should they know about using vocabulary?

Working from texts

If we want children in primary schools to become informed and enthusiastic speakers, readers and writers, we believe that we must firmly ground the language work we do in texts, both making them and sharing them. Something happens when we become immersed in the meaning of a text that goes beyond the study of isolated words or sentences. Outside the confines of a linguistics department of a university there are few of us who find the prospect of studying the uses of the '-ing' participle, or the phoneme /f/, more enticing than, for example, the following:

> A hooded figure came swiftly down the front steps of the castle. Clearly not wanting to be seen, it walked as fast as possible towards the Forbidden Forest. Harry's victory faded from his mind as he watched. He recognized the figure's

prowling walk. Snape, sneaking into the forest while everyone else was at dinner – what was going on?

(Rowling 1997: 165)

We are not claiming that it will necessarily be narrative that will engage every reader's interest. The kinds of enjoyment to be had from reading texts, and the range of uses too, are almost limitless, and it has been exciting over the last few years to see the exclusive emphasis on story reading, and story writing, widening in primary schools. Some readers' attention will be attracted by a passage like this:

Different dinosaurs lived at different times and many of the best known dinosaurs never actually met. For example, no Tyrannosaurus rex ever tried to kill a Stegosaurus because their existence was separated by about eighty million years.

(Bingham 2009: 4)

Texts, whether written or spoken, offer us opportunities to indulge our interests – to gossip about the neighbours, or find out more about life in England as Jane Austen saw it, or about how to grow chrysanthemums for that matter.

How are texts constructed?

The aim of all primary teaching, not just that loosely labelled 'English', must be to help pupils to become more powerful participators in text making and text sharing. But for this to happen, they must delve into language below the text level, must find out more about how the resources of the language enable us to package and present meaning in interesting and varied ways. Children can be shown how writers learn to exploit the possibilities of syntax, that is, the rules for constructing sentences for a range of purposes. Words can be used literally or figuratively. They don't just label aspects of experience but bring with them a wealth of cultural, social and personal associations. And those words are built up from the forty-four or so phonemes that comprise the sounds of English. Learning about the graphemes, or combinations of letters of the alphabet that enable those sounds to be written down, will help children to get to grips with aspects of the language system.

'Top-down' or 'bottom-up' approaches to language work?

How do you think work on the language system should be tackled in the primary school? Does effective language work, whether we are thinking about literacy or oracy (speaking and listening), start from texts and work down from there to studying the smaller units of language? This could be described as a 'top-down' approach. Or is the reverse more effective – a 'bottom-up' approach – especially in Key Stage 1? This would place an emphasis on, in the Early Years at least, decoding and encoding letters and words.

When it comes to planning each individual lesson, of course, a teacher will have a variety of starting points. Our argument in pleading for some daily *text-based* work is that children are in the first instance more likely to be attracted by the prospect of meaning making or sharing before getting down to the nitty-gritty of how the meaning making is done. For instance:

- A reception teacher may share a text with the class, having chosen it because of the predominance of /s/ sounds that can be heard in it.
- A Year 4 teacher might tell the class: 'We're going to be considering persuasive writing this week. I've got a text that I want us to look at together.' She might then decide to look at some of the vocabulary as a detailed focus for the first lesson, perhaps later moving on to how the text is constructed, before suggesting that the children write one themselves.

The views of three first-year students

It might be interesting before reading further to compare your current views about the kinds of language knowledge you feel you need with those of some other students. Barbara, Katie and Lynne are first-year students on a three-year teacher training course. When these discussions took place they had been in college for only two or three weeks. We want to focus in particular on some of their thoughts about the teaching of reading.

Barbara

Barbara is 36 years old. She has two children aged ten and eight and has worked for four years in a playgroup. Her thinking about language has been influenced by this work, and especially by watching her elder son, Graham, learn to read. She shared lots of stories with Graham and felt that before he started school he was very enthusiastic about books. During his first year at school a lot of emphasis was placed by his teacher on phoneme/grapheme relationships – on what are referred to as 'decoding' procedures. This process seemed to him to be very slow and he began to lose some of his initial enthusiasm and even to turn away from books. At this stage in her thinking, therefore, Barbara would emphasise the importance in the Early Years of teachers sharing texts with children, to carry on the enjoyment they have already experienced at home, or, if they have not been so fortunate, to introduce them to the pleasures of reading.

Katie

Katie is 23 years old. Before coming to college she completed A-level courses in English literature and language and general studies and was then in full-time work. She has one son, Kim, aged three. She agrees with Barbara about the importance of instilling in children a love of books and reading. However, she makes a distinction between the roles of parents and teachers. She sees it as the responsibility of the teacher, from the Early Years on, to turn the child into an independent reader. This would mean the child learning how to decode, how to build the smallest units of language, graphemes, into words, and then words into sentences and so on. In the meantime, whilst this is happening, it is the job of the parents to share books with their children, keeping the love of reading alive until such time as they can read for themselves. She feels that it is the media that have influenced her in her thinking about reading.

Lynne

Lynne is 20 years old. She has no children and so far has had little or no regular contact with any. She came on to a teacher training course after studying A-level courses in politics and communications and then working in publishing for two years. She too feels that she has been heavily influenced by the media in her current thinking about reading. In Lynne's view, little can be done to turn children into readers until they have been given the knowledge of how to read independently. Like Katie, it seems sensible to Lynne to start with the smallest units of language, the phonemes, or sounds, which have been converted to letters on the page, and to give the children decoding strategies in the Early Years.

These were quite brief conversations and the three students were concentrating mainly on 'how to help children to start reading'. We think there might have been similar differences in emphasis if we had asked them to consider what children need to do next, after those initial reading stages have been achieved. We are quite sure also that if writing had been the topic for discussion, a range of views would have emerged from the group. We would expect some of them at this early stage in their training to hold a 'bottom-up' view of writing. By this we mean that they would emphasise the importance of starting from the smallest units of language, teaching children to make the letter shapes. This parallels the idea of starting to read by decoding the marks on the page, the letters of the alphabet in their various combinations. Other people would feel that it was important to ask children, from the very beginning, to write texts of all kinds, even though the texts might be indecipherable until the children had learned the rudiments of making the letters and combining them into words. Where do you stand at present on these issues?

The great literacy debate – conflicting views

Our experience as teacher trainers has been that more prospective teachers start their courses by holding a 'bottom-up' view than a 'top-down' one. The media are to some extent responsible for this, as Katie and Lynne both mentioned. In recent years, articles in the press have vilified what they call 'trendy, modern approaches' to the teaching of reading and have hailed a perceived return to phonics with enthusiasm. We think there is more to it than media pressure, however. We have the feeling that, viewed from many an adult's perspective, at least as far as Key Stage 1 children are concerned, to start from the smallest units seems extremely logical. How can children read until they know what the letters 'say'? How can they write until they can form the shapes of the letters? The Rose review has come out strongly in favour of this approach to the teaching of reading and has made it clear that synthetic phonics should be taught by means of a structured programme in 'relatively short, discrete daily sessions' (Rose 2006: 16). This does not suggest, then, that text-based work must be abandoned.

'It is widely agreed', says Rose, 'that phonic work is an essential part, but not the whole picture, of what it takes to become a fluent reader and skilled writer' (Rose 2006: 20). So, we would urge, there must still be room in the day for the sharing of whole texts, not just for the sheer enjoyment of it, not just to foster positive attitudes to literacy, though both of these are vital, but because texts themselves, if they are carefully chosen, support children in becoming readers. Good text-based literacy learning has very little to do with inferring from the pictures what the word is that the reader is trying to decode. Good, supportive texts for beginner readers will have a clear, repetitive structure that encourages children to join in with shared reading, and behave like readers, do what readers do, at the same time as they are applying their developing phonic skills.

Take, for example, *Look Out, Suzy Goose* by Petr Horacek (2008). Suzy is tired of the company of the other noisy geese and wants to find some peace and quiet. Her big feet go 'flip, flop' as she sets off on her quest. And they continue to go 'flip' and 'flop' as she ventures further. These words can easily be decoded phonemically, but they can also be remembered by those who find phonics difficult at first. Suzy soon attracts some undesirable attention, and after a few shared readings children will enjoy predicting the words that are to come over the page – because they refer to some evil characters like 'fox' and 'wolf'. Words such as 'pad, pad' and 'creep, creep' and 'tiptoe, tiptoe' are repeated alongside 'flip, flop'. Will silly Suzy make it back to the company of the others? This story, and very many others like it, help to make clear what the business of reading is all about. A short, discrete daily session of sharing texts like these is at the heart of teaching children to read.

Learning to read is not simple. Children are able to bring to it a diverse range of skills, tactics and experiences, some of them acquired as speakers or as singers of nursery rhymes. Skilled teachers will know when to tap into the children's phonic knowledge and when to refer to other knowledge they know the child has, to support them in decoding the text. The difficulty with sounds (phonemes) is that they are decontextualised. To some children they must seem to have little or nothing to do with reading. This is especially true for children who find it difficult to hear the constituent sounds in a word. And this is a particularly difficult thing to do in English, which is not a phonetic language. An important, perhaps the important, message of this book is that language knowledge which is decontextualised is not of very much use to anyone, teachers or children. This is as true at the upper end of the primary school as it is in Key Stage 1. For example, we talked in Chapter 1 about some children who had been given lists of conjunctions, but who found it very difficult to use this knowledge in the context of their own writing.

Language systems must support language processes!

Teachers who introduce children to isolated bits of knowledge, such as the three sounds in 'hat' or what a conjunction is, or, for that matter, what an autobiography is or what constitutes a title page, will not benefit their pupils unless they can help them to build this information into coherent and ever more detailed and sophisticated approaches to speaking, reading and writing. Perhaps the most fundamental aspect of language knowledge for primary teachers to acquire therefore is how to make language knowledge at each level – text, sentence and word – inform understanding at the other levels. They must know how to work from the top levels of the system down, and from the bottom, from the smallest units, up.

Reconciling opposing viewpoints

There is nothing new about multi-strategy approaches to speaking, reading and writing. You may have met teachers who have been practising them successfully for many years. The National Curriculum makes it clear that this is the correct approach. In this extract from the programme of study for reading at Key Stage 1 (DfEE/QCA 1999: 46), top-down and bottom-up reading cues are listed:

Within a balanced and coherent programme, pupils should be taught to use the following knowledge, understanding and skills:

Phonemic awareness and phonic knowledge	*These two talk about learning the smallest*
Word recognition and graphic knowledge	*bits of language, words and sounds and so are 'bottom up'.*
Grammatical awareness	*These two refer to picking up cues from*
Contextual understanding	*sentences and whole texts and so are 'top down'.*

If we turn to the programmes of study for writing at Key Stage 1 (DfEE/QCA 1999: 48), we read that pupils should be taught:

- to assemble and develop ideas on paper and on screen;
- to write extended texts with support.

At the same time as they are doing this:

- they should be taught to use capital letters, full stops, question marks and to begin to use commas;
- they should be taught to write each letter of the alphabet;
- they should be taught to spell common words.

Perhaps there are still some diehard exclusively 'top-downers' and 'bottom-uppers' about, but if so it is high time for them to each forsake their respective corners and meet in the middle of the ring. We have made plain our own feeling that the 'top' level, the text level, is crucial in enticing children to venture further into language study. However, we need to go much further than we have sometimes done in the past to help children to understand how texts, both written and spoken, are constructed and the significance of the syntactic, lexical and phonemic choices speakers and writers have available to them to help them put their spoken and written messages across.

Good classroom practice

You will see that we find it impossible to separate thoughts about language knowledge for primary teachers from considering the ways in which such knowledge will be presented to children in the primary classroom. To separate them might be to allow our readers to fall into the very trap we are urging all teachers to avoid, of acquiring decontextualised language information that is quickly forgotten or meaningless to the learner. We know because we have fallen into this trap ourselves. We realised that many of our students had little or no knowledge of grammar and we allowed ourselves to be panicked into planning some very decontextualised grammar sessions. We learned our lesson when one of the students observed at the end of one of these: 'I now know what a finite verb is, but I have nowhere to put it in my head.' We very much hope that no reader who perseveres to the end of the book will find themselves in this position.

Using this book

We have emphasised the importance in the classroom of relating work at each language level to work at all the other levels. Chapters 9 and 10 explore these relationships with reference to four fiction and poetry texts and four non-fiction texts respectively. Chapters 11 and 12 explore non-book and electronic texts and digital communication texts respectively. For readers who are struggling to come to terms with the kinds of language knowledge encompassed by each of these levels, we thought it might be helpful to write about texts, sentences and words separately. We have done this in Chapters 4, 5, 6, 7 and 8. However, before starting this more detailed exploration of aspects of the language system, we want to look briefly at the significance for our language framework of what children have learned about language before they come to school.

Summary

In this chapter we have discussed:

- the importance of grounding language work firmly in whole texts;

- how texts are composed of patterns of smaller units of language: sentences, words and sounds;

- relating the 'big shape' of the whole text to the smaller units in ways that are meaningful to children;

- the importance of avoiding decontextualised language knowledge.

3

Building on preschool children's language knowledge

One of the more persistent themes to have run through the last five decades at least is the myth of the children who 'have no language'. The origins of this belief are too complex to trace in detail here. Often, the idea seems to have originated in a misreading of the work of Basil Bernstein. Almost always it was, indeed often still is, children from families of low socio-economic status who are labelled like this. What is frequently meant when such judgements are made is not that the children are literally dumb, but that they don't behave linguistically as their teachers would like them to. Language is acquired in a specific context. For most children this means first of all in their own homes, amongst parents and other caregivers. Sometimes children find the classroom a very different context for talk, and one that is not so supportive.

Language learning starts at home

All children, except for those with an exceptional degree of handicap, a gross defect of intelligence or a severe impairment of hearing, come to school having learned a great deal of language. This is true regardless of their social class. We can find evidence for this in Gordon Wells' (1987) fifteen-year longitudinal study of 128 children across the social spectrum in Bristol. Wells studied the tasks that children can achieve through talk, such as:

- asking questions;
- making plans;
- recalling past events;
- commenting on the world around them.

He also looked at the range of meanings they could make while carrying out those tasks, and the linguistic shape of their utterances. The findings of the research suggested that all the children, when recorded in their homes over a period extending from their first to their fifth birthdays, seemed to be learning in the same sort of way. By the end of this first phase of the research, for each child all the major linguistic systems were more or less in place. The children knew, for example:

- how to formulate questions in a variety of ways;
- how to form past tenses;
- how to phrase requests in a way that was likely to get a positive response.

Each child had a vocabulary of several thousand words. All this is miraculous enough in itself if one considers that they were only just about five years old and had had few, if any, specific 'language lessons'. What is truly awesome is that some children at this age have already begun to operate in more than one language. Gordon Wells, who has a nice way with metaphors, describes this early feat of learning as 'a sheer climb up the face of a cliff' (Wells 1987: 32). It seems regrettable therefore that education research has repeatedly drawn attention to the language failings of some children. We do need to remind ourselves constantly of how much they have in fact achieved.

How do children learn to talk?

Over the last forty years at least researchers (psycholinguists this time and not educationalists) have approached this question from a variety of angles, leading to some quite famous 'fallings out' between them. We will try in this chapter to focus on those aspects that have a particular bearing on the job of primary teachers, especially in Key Stage 1, as they strive to build on what has already been achieved by the children so far.

Chomsky: the Language Acquisition Device (LAD)

It is possible to see language learning as innate, part of a child's genetically transmitted inheritance, like walking upright or using the hands as tools. It was Chomsky who emphasised this approach. He suggested that inside the brain of each one of us is something called a Language Acquisition Device, or LAD for short, which predisposes us to learn and to use language. This is important to bear in mind if you have been inclined to take the view that children learn to speak by imitating adults. Of course, they do learn from the adults around them, but there is more to language learning than this. This is most obviously true when children say things that they have never heard an adult say. Examples might be:

- I runned all the way to school today.
- There are some sheeps in the school field.

These children have learned the general rule for forming the past tense, or for turning singular nouns into plural ones, and they are over-applying it to irregular examples.

No budgerigar or parrot, learning by imitation only, would ever do this. Children appear to seek the underlying principles that will account for the patterns they recognise in their language experiences. Adults, in their interactions with children, continually offer them new evidence of how things are done, and the children incorporate that evidence into their own developing language systems. They then use their systems to interact with the adults, they make errors, saying things the adult does not recognise as part of the 'mature' system, and then new evidence is given to the children that enables them to modify their original hypotheses. So one could say that in the first few years of life children are progressively reconstructing the language of their communities, on the basis of evidence from the more mature members of them. Wells (1987: 51) quotes Andrew Locke in calling this 'the guided reinvention of language'.

Vygotsky and Bruner: social aspects of language learning

Vygotsky and Bruner, outstanding among many other researchers, have emphasised that adults and older children have a vital role to play at all stages in the development of babies' language. Chomsky himself stressed that it is the experience of being in a language-using environment that triggers the innate 'languaging mechanisms' in children. But even a stimulating environment is not enough. The image of children as being like plants, put into fertile soil and provided with an encouraging climate and then left to grow as and how they will, has probably been harmful to some children's progress, and has possibly prevented many from reaching their full potential. Many so-called 'privileged' children have their own spaces to play in, and are provided with televisions, computers, video games and so on. Yet in terms of their language development these things are not necessarily of very much help to them. What young children need is first-hand language experience: as much interaction as they can get, with adults and with older children, one-to-one or in small groups, engaging in topics of shared interest and encouraging an ever-extending range of purposes for talk.

The role of adults in language learning

Wells' research suggested that the quantity of language experienced by preschool children is a crucial factor; there is a clear relation between the children's rate of progress and the amount of language they experience with their parents and other adults. All the children who Wells studied made progress, but those who experienced less conversation progressed at a slower rate.

Another of Wells' findings in this area should give teachers food for thought, especially those in nursery and reception classes. He concluded that, to be most helpful, children's experiences of conversation should be in one-to-one situations, with the adults talking about matters of interest and concern to the children. Both adults and children should be paying attention to the same objects or events. In the home, it is frequently the child who initiates the conversations, and a supportive adult does their best to interpret situations in ways indicated by the child, though this is often difficult, even if the adult is very familiar with the child's ways of thinking and talking. It is vitally important to try to build shared structures of meaning.

The earliest stages of language learning

Preschool children, though they can cope well with conversation given the kinds of supportive adults described above, frequently do not have the conversational sophistication to deal with talking to people outside their social circle. They have acquired their language knowledge in very specific contexts, in daily, repeated activities such as washing and dressing, eating and going for walks to the shops and to other familiar places. They are particularly fortunate if these daily contexts have included adults singing songs and reciting nursery rhymes with them, sharing books, especially stories, or playing pretend games, such as sailing away on the sofa to a treasure island, stiff with pirates.

Babblings

Halliday (1973) has pointed out that, when children first begin to 'talk' about things, and they do this, in a sense, even in the first few weeks of life, they use a language that bears no resemblance to that of any adult. You may think it odd to use the word 'language' about these early babblings at all. Yet children at this stage are indeed acquiring control over their 'sound-making apparatus', though it is true that all babies make more or less the same range of sounds, regardless of their nationality. Adults, in one of their very first interventionist roles, then come along and reinforce the sounds they recognise as being part of their own 'phonemic set'. At first, babies have no sense of language as being for communicating with others, but, the more this significant role for language becomes apparent, the more they want to share sounds with those around them. This is a vital stage in children's development as meaning makers and sharers. From this point on, they begin to have an inkling of how language can serve these purposes.

The sounds that are encouraged and repeated by the adults in a child's world are maintained and become ever more systematised and organised, and the others die away. Of course, the sounds that adults reinforce are those that they recognise as the sounds of the language or languages they speak themselves: English or Welsh, for example. 'Phoneme' is the technical term for one of these sounds. In English, there are approximately forty-four such sounds. The number is approximate because the sounds that speakers use vary slightly depending on their accents.

Once they have reached this stage, children have a 'two-tier' language system. They can make meanings, which are sometimes decipherable by those who know them well and share their lives. They do this by building up a system of sounds, or phonemes, which becomes ever more closely related to the sound system that those around them are using. Adults are very keen indeed to get at the meanings their children are trying to make, and an adult will frequently ascribe meaning to a child's utterance based on their adult understanding. The whole process is 'meaning driven'. The meanings are not just related to obtaining sustenance, though this must be very important to babies. Halliday identified at least five other purposes for 'speaking' in a one-year-old child he studied. These include:

- language for creating imaginary happenings;

- language for finding things out;
- language for joining in a range of collaborative activities with the adults and others around them.

The informative function of language

It is interesting to note that Halliday found that one function developed quite a while after the others, at 22 months – interesting because this is the function that dominates adults' thinking about language and use of language. This is the informative, or 'I've got something to tell you', function. Halliday feels that the idea that language can be used as a means of communicating information to someone who does not already possess that information is a very sophisticated one. It depends on the internalisation of a complex set of linguistic concepts that young children do not possess. It's the only function that depends entirely on an exchange of words. It is often hard for even the most supportive adult to be sure what a child wants to tell them, sometimes a child as old as four or five years.

Increasing vocabulary and syntax

With ever greater, though frequently not total, control of the sound system within their reach, children can go on, with adult encouragement, to build a vocabulary of several thousand words before they are five years old. And slowly they gain control of the last tier of the adult 'languaging system'. This is the ability to combine words, using the rules of syntax, so that they can make meanings in increasingly flexible ways. Semantics (knowledge of how to make meanings), sounds, words and syntax are now all in place.

Early language learning: its significance for primary teachers

A number of points about these learning processes are important for primary teachers. Most important of all is the emphasis given by researchers such as Halliday and Wells to children as active meaning makers, originally creating their own systems for making meaning without any thought as to whether they are understood or not. The concept of language as a shared social system, outside themselves as it were, and waiting to be acquired by them, becomes a focus of their attention only in gradual stages. Not all children will learn the shared system at the same rate, although most will have learned the fundamentals before starting school. We are concerned that the increased emphasis on teaching aspects of the language system, even at the lower end of Key Stage 1, will put unhelpful pressure on children who are still working their way towards full use of it, though they are by no means inarticulate children. Society expects teachers to help children to learn this system at all four levels – semantics, syntax, vocabulary and sounds.

We hope by now, however, you will understand why we have continued to emphasise meaning making and sharing as the best language starting point in school, with the learning of phonemes, vocabulary and syntax serving the ends of the meaning making and not the other way round. Robin Alexander (2008: 12) stresses the important role that we have gradually come to understand that talk has in contributing to effective learning: 'The new approach demands both pupil engagement *and* teacher intervention. And the principal means by which pupils actively engage and teachers constructively intervene is through talk.' Alexander goes on to share another fascinating insight, gleaned from neuroscientific research. He makes it clear that talk is necessary not just for learning but also for the building of the brain itself as a physical organism. And the period that coincides with primary schooling is the very one in which the brain in effect restructures itself. During the years between 3/4 and 10/11 the brain's volume quadruples, and talk actively and vigorously fuels these processes.

Learning the language system: contrasting parental attitudes

Should we expect children, even in the Early Years Foundation Stage, to have a metalanguage, a language for talking about language? It makes a lot of sense to be able to discuss aspects of the language system, once we are sure that children are ready for this. To be able to talk about language helps children to see it as an artefact, as something external to themselves, which can be thought about independently of using it to accomplish particular purposes in particular contexts. Some children have been prepared by their parents for this way of thinking by the way in which the parents have supported their children's language acquisition. Parents whose own lives involve a lot of reading and writing are more likely to be aware of language as a socially constructed system, external to the individual child, and which he or she must therefore be inducted into. They may therefore set about teaching their children this system by breaking it down into differently sized chunks, such as words and sentences, and then 'putting these under the microscope'. They are likely to believe that language can be taught to children.

Other parents seem to adopt an approach closer to the image of the child as 'a plant in a well-manured garden', which we referred to earlier. Shirley Brice-Heath (1983), who has carried out interesting research into these contrasting parental attitudes, characterises these parents' views as 'No use me telling him – he just gotta learn.'

Bruner (1983) points out that some parents introduce books to their children with the idea of using them as a way of teaching their children to talk. In other words, the parents are keen to extend their children's vocabulary, especially with regard to the words for the names of objects or 'nouns'. It may well be counterproductive for parents or teachers to introduce aspects of the language system too early: the end result might be to discourage their children's attempts to get to grips with it themselves.

Learning the language system: classroom approaches

Teachers as well as parents need to be very careful that children are not parroting bits of learning that are in fact quite meaningless to them. In one early literacy training video, a reception class are sharing the book *The Jigaree* with their teacher, and a child is asked the name of the letter that starts the word 'Jigaree'. 'Jade', he replies, perhaps drawing on his knowledge of the names of children in the school. The task for the primary teacher is to be sensitive to those children who have reached the stage at which they can see the language as a system, those who are coming up to this, and those who as yet cannot distance themselves from the job of work that the language is doing for them.

This is admittedly a tall order for a teacher in a busy class of some thirty children – not only to recognise these various stages but also to provide differentiated support for each group. You can at least resolve to look for significant signs of progress. For example, if you plan to teach in nursery or reception classes you should be on the lookout for children who use words to refer to mental processes. By this we mean words and phrases such as 'I wonder what . . .', 'I think I know what . . .', 'Let's pretend . . .' When you are sharing stories with children, you may find that only some of them can point out that a character in a story 'said X, but really he meant Y'. Children who can do these things have come to some objective understanding of language as a means of intending, thinking, knowing, planning, pretending, remembering, doubting – lying, even. And they know too that these activities can be talked about. They will vary in the speed at which they arrive at these realisations.

Language learning takes time!

Where teachers have perhaps sometimes gone wrong is in forgetting that we are sensitive to the best kinds of language learning we have described in this chapter, but we talk about them as 'a starting point'. Yet we have seldom, if ever, been on an in-service course entitled 'Language Development: Phase Two', let alone 'Phase Three' or 'Phase Four'. Occasionally, we have attended courses on so-called 'advanced reading skills', which turned out not to be about skills used by advanced readers. What has been described in this chapter is only a beginning, though a very impressive one, and one that may take some children quite a while to complete. The sophistication of text, syntax and vocabulary choices that the English language makes available is still to be discovered by five year olds who have at least eleven years of compulsory schooling ahead of them. We have possibly not done enough in the past to ensure that all children explore the possibilities that language offers, especially in their writing, but also in their reading and speaking. The rest of this book will be concerned with exploring some of the intricacies of this fascinating system, at each of these three levels, starting with text.

Summary

In this chapter we have discussed:

- the impressive amount of language learning that takes place before children start school;

- Chomsky's notion of a Language Acquisition Device and Vygotsky and Bruner's emphasis on the social aspects of learning;

- Halliday's range of language functions;

- contrasting parental attitudes to developing children's language;

- the importance of sensitive teaching in order to take children on from what has already been achieved at home.

Texts, sentences and words

4

Some characteristics of texts

What exactly is a 'text'? We have used the term several times already in previous chapters, and if you are a mature entrant to teacher training – and possibly even if you are not – it may not be a term that you remember from your school days. The word 'text' in this book is being used to refer to complete and coherent passages of spoken or written language that come about because people live in social groups or communities and language is essential to them in living their lives. Each time someone, or a group of people, sets out with the intention of carrying out a job of work that involves making or sharing verbal meaning in some way, they are creating a text. This might include:

- writing a report on a visit;
- describing how to make a pancake;
- gossiping with friends about the day's events.

Texts fulfil our purposes by allowing us to explore and express aspects of meaning in subjects we are concerned with or interested in. Sometimes the making of the text is an end in itself: we create it for the pleasure of the making and sharing. This probably applies to most stories and poems, or to the gossip we mentioned just now. Sometimes reading or writing a text is a means to something else – getting a new job, or having pancakes for dinner. Texts are produced with audiences or readers in mind, although, as, for example, in the case of a private diary, these readers may be the creators of the texts themselves. We shall see later that the image we have of the people who are to receive our texts exerts some influence on the ways in which we go about constructing the meaning in them.

'Text' is a useful term because it embraces all those many and varied ways of encapsulating meaning, formal and informal, that can be readily observed in use in every aspect of twenty-first-century society. 'Written texts' are of course not synonymous with 'books'. A book may contain within it several different types of text. Written texts can take the form of road signs or bus tickets or seed packets or chocolate bar wrappers. Frequently, diagrams, photographs, drawings and so on form an important part of how the meaning is created in these texts. It is important to develop the interest that even very young children show in environmental print (a generic term for all the kinds of written texts encountered in their homes and neighbourhoods). Children's first questions will probably be about what the text is for, but they will soon go on to develop an interest in how the text is constructed. Try, for example, if you live near one of these, asking them whether it's true that their local supermarket is labelled 'Sainsbury's'. We are sure you'll be put right! Examples like this should indicate to us that we need have no fear of discussing the choices of vocabulary and syntax that speakers and writers make when constructing a text, even with very young children. Once children's interest has been engaged by the subject matter, they can very willingly be engaged in discussing text structure.

Texts can be written or spoken. These days those are not the clear-cut distinctions they once were, although writers and speakers still find themselves contending with contrasting contexts and conditions in putting their texts together. As well as taking part in face-to-face interactions, most of us now use the telephone regularly, creating a different kind of spoken text. When we are e-mailing each other, are we drawing on our knowledge of how to participate in a speech event, or are we constructing a piece of writing? Our words will certainly appear, not on a piece of paper but on a screen, as will much else of what we read these days. Scrolling skills are now as much a part of reading texts as knowing where to start reading on the printed page. The degree of care we take in composing the e-mail will largely depend on its purpose and on our relations with the participant.

The differences between spoken and written texts

Spontaneous talk

In face-to-face talk situations, each speaker learns to make lightning reactions to what the other speakers are saying and to adjust his or her next utterance accordingly. Sometimes these adjustments are not so slick, and everyone talks at once, or people interrupt each other. Sometimes there are brief silences. If you ever have the opportunity to make a study of spontaneous conversation, one of the interesting things you might observe is how long a group of people who are engaged in constructing a spoken text together – for example a friendly chat in the college bar – can tolerate silence. It's also interesting to note who takes on the task of 'filling the gap'. In some talk situations, such as a college lecture or an interview in a police station, the task of making sure that the discussion moves along is allocated to an individual person, by virtue of their role, though he or she may decide to pass the responsibility on to someone else. Primary children, at least once they are past reception, have relatively few opportunities to introduce a topic for discussion in a classroom. They are usually put in the position of responding to a teacher's comments or questions, though in Wells' research they were frequently observed to ask a question or start a conversation at home.

Rehearsed talk

Spoken texts such as monologues and sermons are constructed by one speaker. Many but by no means all of these are likely to have been planned to a greater or lesser extent before being delivered. Some may have been rehearsed. This planning is likely to result in the text having more of the characteristics of writing in its syntax and vocabulary. Indeed, in some cases, faced, say, with the prospect of giving a talk to a very large, unknown audience, many of us would perhaps write down what we wanted to say, though even then, as we warmed to the task of delivering the speech, we might depart from the script and improvise a little from time to time.

Spontaneous writing

Of course, it would be a mistake to assume that just because a text is a written one it will have been carefully planned. Some writing is practically as spontaneous as some speech; a note pinned to the fridge door saying, 'Gone to meating: back at 8', does not tax our powers of composition very much. Even if we feel a touch of uncertainty about the spelling of the third word, we are extremely unlikely to make ourselves late for the meeting by stopping to get out the dictionary. It really doesn't matter; our nearest and dearest either will not notice, or, if they do, will hopefully put the mistake down to haste or a stressful day.

Writing that is planned and drafted

On very many occasions writers will go to great lengths to strive for correctness in written texts, not only in spelling, grammar and punctuation, but also in the construction of the text itself. We may try to look at some other texts, similar to the ones we are trying to create. We may ask someone to read through a text before submitting it to its intended audience. Does it 'sound right'? The interesting question then arises: How does the person we consult know whether it sounds right or not? How, for that matter, do we know how to participate in that conversation in the college bar without putting people's backs up or becoming a social misfit?

How do we learn what we know about text creation?

The answers to this question take us back to the learning processes undertaken by babies and young children, which we described in Chapter 3. In that chapter, we referred to a crucial moment in all babies' language development when they become aware that the language they have been evolving for themselves can, if they make some adjustments to it, be used to share meanings with those around them. They have discovered, in other ways, that language is a social system. The adults and older children around them do all they can to introduce them to aspects of the system they use themselves. Young children are helped in very special ways:

- aspects of the system, such as sentence length, may be simplified;
- significant words, especially nouns, are isolated;
- these words are spoken in a very clear tone directed specifically to the children while the objects referred to are present;
- sometimes explicit language 'lessons' are provided by parents.

We were keen to emphasise in that chapter that young children themselves take a lot of responsibility for their own learning. As they participate in creating spoken texts with those around them, they take the data that the more experienced speakers offer to them and experiment with them, receiving feedback to help them to correct their mistakes. In this way they bring all aspects of their language ever closer to the ways in which the people around them are using language. To a very large extent, this is how we go on learning to create texts, though the contexts for learning change in crucial ways as we get older.

Control over text creation

We have described already in Chapter 3 how tolerance of mistakes decreases, even while children are still very young and inexperienced 'text creators'. Models of how things should be done, and feedback on mistakes, may not always be so readily available, or be offered in a friendly fashion. In his or her own classroom, for example, the teacher almost always assumes the right to define what forms of spoken text are appropriate for the day-to-day management of affairs. Woe betide the child who uses the wrong form of text structure when asking to go to the toilet. To use words deemed 'rude' by a teacher, though they may be taken for granted in a child's home, can lead to some very hostile aspersions being cast on the child in question. It is assumed that we have learned certain 'language ways of the world' by the age of five, more by seven, more still by eleven. These are the ages at which primary children's language development has been tested nationally, and we listed in Chapter 1 some of the language achievements that are expected at these ages. The National Curriculum makes it very clear what spoken and written texts children should be able to produce at each of these stages and what kinds of texts they should be able to read.

How many different kinds of text are there?

Those mature entrants to teacher training we referred to earlier might remember the days when children in primary schools were expected to write their news and stories and, as they got older, to produce 'compositions'. In the 1960s, 'creative writing' was very much in vogue. As we remember it, this frequently involved writing free verse: in some cases, the form the text was to take was left to each child to decide. It would almost certainly turn out to be narrative of some kind. In 1978, an HMI report on Primary Education in England (DES 1978) bemoaned the lack of range in the writing asked for by junior teachers.

During the 1960s and 1970s, teachers' perspective on writing, and on reading, was often a psychological rather than a sociological one. In many classrooms texts were frequently created by asking the children to employ one or more of their five senses, or in some cases to 'use their imagination' to produce a 'personal response' to a stimulus such as a piece of music, or a walk through the woods on a snowy morning. Where the language knowledge came from to enable these texts to be created was not so closely scrutinised. Clearly children acquired some knowledge from their reading, but, as a great deal of emphasis was placed on originality, teachers did not want to see too much evidence of the reading material having been used as a model. Similarly, it was not considered to be a good idea to encourage children to act as writing response partners for each other in case one ended up with several pieces of very similar work.

The social origins of texts

Attitudes to text creation have now largely swung away from this emphasis on the isolated, soul-searching young writer. There is an important shift in emphasis away from an individual search for personal meaning towards groups of people helping each other to define and refine what it is they want to say. Teachers are now more aware of children having needs as writers that are very similar to those of any other writers in the world outside the classroom: need for time to plan and revise their work, to seek advice and positive comment on what they are producing and, perhaps most importantly, to look for models of how these writing tasks are carried out.

There is now a greater awareness that the writing of certain types of texts, such as 'news' and stories, was over-emphasised in schools, whilst other text types, frequently the ones that feature most prominently in the adult world, were almost entirely absent. The National Curriculum made it legally binding on all schools to ensure that children both read and write texts of many kinds, not just stories and poems. The vagueness of 'composition' disappeared and has been replaced by specific lists of text types. Children are entitled to learn more about the variety of types of reading and writing (and speaking too) that their society values and finds interesting and worthwhile.

The changing needs of society

Central to the view of language we are building in this book is the image of the thinking, reflecting individual, located in a particular culture, at a particular time, and participating in reading, writing and speaking to others, at home, at work and in a variety of other social situations. Increasingly complex demands may be made on this person as he or she participates in creating texts or reading texts. We cannot know for certain what these demands will be in later life for today's five to 11 year olds. Society is constantly changing in its needs, attitudes, expectations and values. Texts change, as do styles of dress, modes of transport, attitudes to eating meat, and so much else. So even a text type such as a recipe or a report must be seen as fluid and constantly evolving. At any one point in time, groups and individuals within a society vary in their willingness to tolerate innovation, or what they define as departures from the norm. If you fail to fill in a blank cheque along the lines laid down by your bank, it's unlikely that you will be given any money. At the other extreme, in many of the verbal arts, especially in poetry and songwriting, or story writing, innovation is expected and is considered desirable. And there are many 'grey areas' in between. The kind of text we are writing now is perhaps one of them. You may be surprised to see sentences beginning with 'and'. You may feel irritated by our use of 'we' and 'you', or elided forms such as 'won't'. Perhaps you have been brought up to believe that these syntactic and vocabulary choices are more appropriate in spoken than in written texts. (It is possible of course that the publisher was irritated too and has edited out these features at a later stage in producing the book!)

As primary teachers, we can help our pupils to cope by encouraging them to see texts as more than just, as Wray and Lewis (1997: 105) put it, 'transparent conveyers of meaning'. Texts are constructed in the way they are because speakers and writers have made certain language choices. When they are constructing a text, writers or speakers may be affected by some features of their physical context, such as the surroundings, the temperature, the degree of comfort or discomfort they are feeling. For example, spontaneous face-to-face interaction calls for rapid decisions about what to say next. Many written texts, on the other hand, are produced in circumstances that provide opportunities for reflection and revision. Texts are written or spoken in moments of anguish, ecstasy, rage and so on. We have referred already to the effect on a composer of text of other people who are present, or who will eventually read the text. A story written for four year olds will look very different from one written for adults. Text shape, layout, syntax and vocabulary are all different.

The most important task for teachers is to help their pupils to find an appropriate voice for what it is they want to say. Adult writers faced with creating a text do not reinvent the wheel. Text types have their origins in particular social occasions and fulfil particular social purposes, and at a general level, when writers or speakers are engaged in similar tasks, there will be some degree of consistency in the language decisions they make. We suspect that the more confident people become in aspects of their 'language lives' the more some of them are prepared to experiment in their eagerness to get their meanings across, even with types of text that appear relatively fixed.

Primary teachers, on the other hand, are usually dealing with the least confident members of society, because they are the youngest and most socially inexperienced. There is no doubt that in the past we have not done enough as teachers, first to give children experience of reading texts that are constructed in different ways, to help to bring to their notice what skilled and experienced writers and speakers have done, and then to help the children to make use of the full range of language choices available to them. Government tests, especially of 11 year olds, have consistently shown that it is in coping with a range of writing tasks, rather than in reading, that children are failing to reach the expected standards. We have suggested one reason already in this chapter for why this might be so: too much attention has traditionally been given to the writing of stories. We would like to return to story writing in a later part of the chapter, but we want to look first in a little more detail at some aspects of non-narrative texts.

Extending the range: issues in creating non-narrative texts

Successive politicians have been keen on urging teachers to 'get back to basics' when teaching children to write. By this they usually seem to mean showing the children how to punctuate a sentence or produce a more legible script. In fact, the most 'basic' problem a writer faces is what to write about, and then, once poised with pen in hand (or seated at the keyboard), how to begin to order one's ideas. The National Curriculum speaks of chronological and 'non-chronological' ordering of ideas, as if these two labels were somehow of the same kind. To order one's ideas chronologically means to put things down more or less in the order in which they happened. This frequently, but by no means always, happens in stories: 'One day . . . suddenly . . . then . . . next . . .' 'Then' is one of the earliest connectives grasped by children and is much overused to handle what has come to be called 'bed-to-bed' writing (when the child describes what happens from getting up in the morning to going to bed at night). A lot of emphasis in primary schools has been placed, quite rightly, on learning from first-hand experience. Visits are made, for example, to the local Roman villa or the local supermarket. In many a classroom, seeds are planted or chickens are hatched. It is not just in narrative that children have frequent resort to chronological writing. The 'bed-to-bed' approach has been employed by children to write about learning experiences such as each of the above, though this may not at all have been the teacher's intention. How else could the tasks have been organised?

Choosing a structure

To speak of 'non-chronological' ordering is not very much help at first sight because it is an umbrella term that merely refers to any text in which the points are not ordered in a time sequence. It is essential for teachers to have experience at first hand of the different ways in which texts can be ordered, so that they have a clear view of the possibilities available when they discuss a writing task with a child. Let us take a visit to a Roman villa as an example. It offers a wealth of writing opportunities that might be shared out around the class. Stories, poems and plays come readily to mind, but we are pursuing non-fiction possibilities here.

Defining a purpose

What might the teacher's learning objectives have been in organising the visit and what kinds of writing will support these learning objectives? Perhaps the domestic life of the Romano-Britons was the major focus, with the children being asked to prepare a wall display or a class book.

An explanatory text

Some children may want to write about how the villa was heated in winter. What is involved in carrying out this writing task successfully?

- The writer must provide an explanation of a process, not so that readers can carry it out themselves, but so that they understand how it was done.
- The points must be presented in a logical sequence, from showing how and where a source of heat is introduced into the villa to explaining how the heat is maintained and disseminated through the rooms.
- It is likely that the writer's task will be helped by the inclusion of drawings or diagrams.

A procedural text

Other children might have been asked to find out about the diet of the people who lived in the villa, and to carry out some research into styles of eating. They will produce a menu for a Roman banquet, with recipes for some of the dishes.

- They will need models for recipe writing.
- Some feedback would be useful on whether their instructions seem clear enough to produce an edible result.

It is likely that their readers would find it helpful, especially if they are actually going to try their hands at some cooking, to have items arranged in list form, in a logical order. Readers of recipes want to be told exactly what to do, especially when poised over a hot stove with hungry guests expecting to be fed.

A report

One of the more demanding writing tasks might be to write about 'What it was like to live in Roman Britain'. This is difficult for a number of reasons. It means scanning quite a lot of aspects of Roman life and then organising them into some sort of logical sequence. One possibility among several might be to have an introductory sentence, such as 'Life was quite pleasant for most people in Roman Britain, though there were some problems'. This would enable the writer to sort out some examples of things that were pleasant and write about them, and then provide some examples of problems.

Textual cohesion

It would be by no means easy to ensure a successful conclusion to all these writing tasks, even if we think for the moment only about potential problems at the text level, which are what we regard as the 'basic' ones. For one thing, readers expect texts to hang together, to appear to be 'all of a piece', unless there is some very good reason for their changing shape partway through. The technical term for this is 'cohesion'. We want to discuss it here at the text level and shall have more to say in subsequent chapters about how writers can maintain cohesion at the sentence and word levels.

The explanatory text

If we are told that we are going to have an explanation of Roman central heating presented to us, we, as mature adult readers and writers, expect the piece to deal with sources of heat, with underground passages, types of tile and so on. Some of these things, rather than people, will turn out to be the subjects of the sentences. We expect these sentences to be presented to us as a series of general statements about how things were done over the period of the Roman occupation. This means that the piece will be in the past tense, but will not deal with any specific date or place. Our 'heating group' may start off well enough with a sentence about how the Romans heated their houses by using an under-floor system, but, given some uncertainty about the more technical details, might soon resort to a chronological account of what they saw. 'We went through some underground passages and then we noticed . . .' This can all too easily turn into full-blown narrative, with an account of how Gary tripped or Samantha got lost. The subjects of the sentences are now themselves, or their friends, and events are related sequentially. The text has lost its cohesion.

The procedural text

The recipe writers, though they may be familiar in a general way with the structure of a recipe, may fail to appreciate everything readers need to know in order to produce roast field mouse (though it's unlikely that the readers will be actually called upon to do so!). How much knowledge about basic cookery skills can be assumed in one's readers? Must they be told every single thing or can some stages in the process be left to their common sense? Judging what the reader can be assumed to know is an important part of any text construction. This applies to what they might know both about the subject and also about reading this type of text (think of a knitting pattern, for example). Writers need to offer just the right number of cues to steer their readers along without either patronising them or baffling them to the point where they abandon the text.

The report text

The greatest danger is perhaps that those faced with writing a report on life in Roman Britain will resort to copying chunks from a reference book. The heating group have some first-hand experience they can refer to after their visit. They may have made notes or sketches. The recipe group have models to look at and will in all probability at least have seen recipes in newspapers. To talk about the quality of life in Britain at the time of the Romans means holding in your head quite a lot of specific examples about homes and clothes and occupations and a great deal else. All of this information has to be sifted and organised by means of some generalising statements: an example might be 'One very good thing about life at this time was the plumbing.' Then some flesh has to be put on these bare bones. Not only that, but disadvantages have to be weighed against advantages and some conclusion reached. Generally speaking, primary teachers should not expect children to be able to make successful generalising statements in non-fiction texts except when these are tightly rooted in some first-hand experience, though in this we would include experience gained in drama or role-play situations. This last group, for example, might first have role-played a group of villa dwellers and discussed what they found pleasant and what irksome about their lives as they 'sat in the bath house'!

Problems of turning experience into words

There are three elements to juggle with in shaping aspects of an experience into a piece of writing: the subject, the writer and the reader. Sometimes it seems inappropriate for writers to be mentioned directly in their finished pieces. On other occasions it is perfectly acceptable for them to present information directly as they saw it, using the first person pronouns 'I' or 'we'. The latter text structure is easier to handle in many ways, especially if the subject is something one is still trying to get to grips with. As regards the readers of the texts, children are frequently in the position of writing texts for people (teachers) who know more about the subject than they do. This does not make it easy for them to decide how much to tell. It is much easier to write texts for people who are genuinely seeking enlightenment or entertainment. Teachers can turn themselves into such readers at various stages in the writing process, and can also help children by making available other types of reader.

There are, of course, other levels of decision making that writers must face. Texts will consist of sentences or phrases and writers or speakers must decide how to structure those. Vocabulary, too, will need careful handling. We will return to these kinds of language choice in later chapters.

Helping children to make text-level decisions

This is not a book about how to teach writing. However, we cannot resist urging teachers to allocate enough time for discussing with children what kind of text they feel would be appropriate on a given occasion. The long years of story writing, or of 'telling what we did', have left their mark on children and they assume – or their parents, who may be trying to help them, assume – that this is what the teacher wants. Again, if the children have had experience of writing mainly narratives, they may suppose, even when asked to search for information in text and to present it factually, that they are expected to invent some of their answer or to embellish the facts in some way. Decisions like this need to be agreed beforehand, or the text that is eventually presented may be unfairly criticised because it bears disappointingly little resemblance to what the teacher had in mind.

The most common forms of non-fiction text

If you are new to teaching you may feel far from confident about your ability to discuss the significant features of a range of texts, particularly non-fiction texts, with a whole class. It may be of some comfort to you to know that researchers who have studied large numbers of texts suggest that many non-fiction texts are written to fulfil one or other of six purposes.

Some texts provide recounts of events the speaker or writer has participated in or has heard about. They are frequently chronologically ordered and, when children produce them, will sometimes describe everything from what the child had for breakfast to being sick in the coach on the way home (what we earlier called 'bed-to-bed' writing). A second large group is of the 'procedural' type, which tells the reader how to do something – cook a roast field mouse, for example. 'Reports' is a label that can be used for texts that deal with 'how things are' (or were, for example in Roman Britain). They require the writer or speaker to deal in generalisations, though probably illustrated with specific examples of the particular phenomenon that is being discussed. A fourth group of non-fiction texts provides explanations of how or why something happens: in our example, how Roman central heating works.

The other two frequently encountered purposes for producing non-fiction, which we did not include in our Roman Britain list, have been found to be texts presenting an argument and texts discussing an issue. As an example of this last category, we might perhaps have included in our list a group of children writing a letter to a newspaper about the lack of amenities provided for tourists at the villa, though this would have taken us rather outside our target of a wall display or a class book.

Writing frames

When we set out to discuss an issue with a group of friends, the textual cohesion we spoke about above is not such an important matter. We expect the talk to range to and fro. We can backtrack easily, by inserting into the conversation something we meant to say earlier. As we talk, we are likely to think of more ideas, and to be prompted by the others to remember things we had forgotten. Someone may take on the role of chair and attempt to keep order, but on many occasions the talk will be a free-for-all, and may indeed become very incoherent.

Constructing written texts can be a much more lonely business, and the demands to organise what we have to say can be much greater. One's gran may be so pleased to get a letter that she doesn't mind what order the points come in, but other readers will be less forgiving. The more formal and abstract the types of text to be constructed, the greater the demands – especially on an inexperienced writer. Response partners are invaluable in this situation but there will still be many occasions when a class may be faced with getting on with a piece of writing without immediate help being available.

Wray and Lewis (1997) suggest offering children an outline structure in the form of a writing frame to support them in the six most frequently occurring non-fiction written forms. The writing frame would suggest to children those stages in the construction of the text that we have already referred to, and might offer some starting phrases, or phrases for linking one stage of the text with the next: 'on the one hand ...' or 'nevertheless ...' or 'I would like to begin by ...' As Wray and Lewis point out, there are many possible writing frames for each of the six broad purposes for writing, and it is important that any frame suggested to children stays flexible and does not become a rigid form. It could be said that a frame should also be regarded like a pair of water wings, with all the dangers of over-dependence that they can produce, and every effort should be made to dispense with its use as quickly as possible. We have seen story frames in various formats used quite frequently, but in fact it is probably with the more complex structures of non-narrative texts that some children need help.

Summary

In this chapter we have discussed:

- definitions of 'text';

- similarities and differences between spoken and written texts;

- the social origins of texts: how children begin to learn what society expects of them as text makers;

- six types of non-fiction text that the National Curriculum requires children to deal with.

5

Making sense of texts

A writer's or speaker's purpose in embarking on a text is almost always to make meaning of some kind or other. Occasionally as when a child is crying in the middle of the night, it's not so much the meanings that are important as that someone is there, and making soothing noises. It needs to be remembered that the meanings we all strive to make are often far from straightforward. We can use language in order to tell lies, or to present a very biased view of events. In a spoken text, speakers will very often have instant feedback on how their meanings are being received, with comments such as 'I don't understand a word of that', or 'Come off it, who are you trying to kid', and so on. They can then try to take further steps, assuming they are allowed to say more.

Writers are not often there to comment on their meanings, but can offer cues to their readers about how they expect or hope their texts to be read. However, just as a group of speakers are interacting with each other to make meaning, so readers will, in a sense, interact with the texts they are reading, and the meanings they take from those texts will depend on some of the factors we have mentioned already: their age, their knowledge of this subject, their experience of this kind of text, their opinion of the writer and so on. It would be a great mistake to think that 'comprehension', or understanding a text, consists of quarrying it for little chunks of meaning that the writer has built into it. As we become used to reading a particular type of text, we build up pleasurable anticipation of what we expect to find; we bring this knowledge and experience to bear in creating the meaning in our own minds, though of course it would be a very poor reader who deliberately ignored the cues the writer has provided. To be a good reader means to set up a dialogue with the text inside one's own head, with the words the writer has provided sparking off pictures, ideas, comparisons and so on.

Reading as an active process

This may be a view of reading that you have not thought about very much before, especially if you were unfortunate enough to have teachers who talked you through a text line by line, or even perhaps gave you dictated notes on its meaning. You may feel that you lack confidence in your ability to interact with the meanings of texts in this way. We hope that you will pursue this approach further. Although most adults, given perhaps some encouragement to read like this, can carry out that 'dialogue in the head', when you come to the point where you are helping primary children to read like this you will need to plan for more active involvement with the texts. One of your most important tasks in teaching reading will be to think about ways of ensuring lively explorations of the meanings of texts with your class. You need to convince the children that it is not the teacher alone who has the key to unlock the meaning; that it's acceptable to disagree over what something means, provided the readers have considered the evidence in front of them.

A range of reading behaviours

There is another important point to bear in mind about describing reading as 'creating meaning in our own minds'. Not only will different readers obtain different meanings from a text, but the same reader, reading on different occasions, will find different meanings. Some texts, including many poems, are a good example of this, with layers of meaning that come to light only after many readings, and after accruing a lot of experience in reading poetry. Of course, it's not always like this. The act of reading is not always concerned with pondering on meaning. No one wants to tease out the meaning of a railway timetable. To have to do so might result in missing the train, or arriving at the wrong destination. We want the writer to guide us, by means of columns, subheadings, large print, or whatever is most helpful, to the part of the text we need, and we will ignore the rest. But to tease out the meaning of a story or a poem is part of the pleasure of reading the text. On these occasions we feel the language of the text, along the skin and in the imagination. We relish the relationship of one part of the text with another, like the movements in a symphony or as when gazing at a painting. We enjoy the feeling of never being really sure whether we have missed something, or whether the writer's cues could have been interpreted differently.

Complex purposes for reading

It is sometimes suggested that the reader goes to non-fiction in order to learn, rather than simply for enjoyment or 'to lose oneself in another world', which many see as the main reasons for reading fiction or poetry. These definitions are simplistic. It is possible to learn something about rivers from reading *The Wind in the Willows*, although this was not Kenneth Grahame's main reason for writing it. It is possible to read a biography (or a DIY manual if you are that way inclined) simply for enjoyment and to lose oneself in the text.

Approaches to the structuring of fiction and non-fiction texts

It is the case that there are some fundamental differences in the way fiction and non-fiction texts are constructed, though even here there are exceptions. A poem or a work of fiction has been conceived as a whole. It is usual to speak of story structure as comprising a beginning, a middle and an end. All texts, of course, inevitably have a beginning, middle and end – even notes to the milkman. What is implied here is that the writer of a story or a poem has paid very close attention to the relationship between the beginning, the middle and the end. To read them in any other order (though some people do insist on reading the end of a story first!) is to do damage to the author's intentions. The relationship between each part adds something to the meaning of the whole.

It is for this reason that it is unfair to a story writer or a poet to take a section of text and study it without also seeing it in its context. It is rather like looking at one water lily in a Monet painting while the rest of the painting is covered up. It is not a meaningless activity, but in trying to make meaning we are not receiving the data the creator of the piece intended us to. As we become more familiar with a writer's or a painter's work, we can appreciate a detail seen in isolation, because we have in our minds our knowledge of the rest of the text on which to draw. Primary-age children, even in Key Stage 2, are not usually in this position.

The relationship of the parts to the whole is not the same in a non-fiction text. Sometimes there is an expectation on the part of the writer that the reader will start at the beginning and read through to the end. Indeed, in a 'process' text such as 'How to Make a Chocolate Cake' it would be very foolish not to do so. Generally, though, it is possible, if one is so inclined, to approach the text in a more piecemeal fashion, and indeed the text itself should support readers in doing just that. Even in a biography, in which the points are likely to be arranged in chronological order as they are in many a story, it may be that readers do not want to know about the person's early life, and will use the chapter headings to guide them to the part of the life that they are interested in. Chapters in turn may be subdivided with clear headings, enabling the reader to skim through, scanning the pages for a useful section.

There is an implication in what we have said about approaches to non-fiction texts that very often, though not always, readers approach them with a question or questions in mind to which they are seeking an answer or more information. They may be interested in the writer's views on an issue, as in a newspaper editorial, or they may want to make something or carry out a particular process. You may find it useful to remind yourself of the six most frequently found forms of non-fiction text that we listed in Chapter 4.

Having fun with meaning

Whatever the type of text, reading should be seen from the earliest stages in a reader's life as a search for meaning. This search can, of course, take all sorts of forms, some of them very lighthearted. Many young children enjoy nonsense texts more than anything, in which the writer may appear to have turned meaning on its head. Recently, we were told about a class of ten year olds, all boys, who were asked at the end of the school year which language activities they had enjoyed the most. Two things were clear favourites. One was some work on alliteration, which you may have tried yourselves. A letter of the alphabet is chosen and, then, starting with 'one' then 'two' and 'three' and so on, followed by their personal choice of words from lists provided in columns labelled 'Adjective', 'Noun', 'Verb' and 'Noun', the boys conjured up such amazing spectacles as 'one winsome whale wondering whether to waltz' and 'two terrible twins twisting twenty twigs'. Another lesson the boys remembered with great enjoyment was when they read this poem:

I saw a Peacock with a fiery tail
I saw a blazing Comet drop down hail,
I saw a Cloud with ivy circled round,
I saw a sturdy Oak creep on the ground,
I saw a Pismire swallow up a whale,
I saw a raging Sea brim full of ale,
I saw a Venice Glass sixteen foot deep,
I saw a Well full of men's tears that weep,
I saw their Eyes all in a flame of fire,
I saw a House as big as the moon and higher,
I saw the Sun even in the midst of night,
I saw the Man that saw this wondrous sight.

(Anon)

What the boys said they enjoyed about the experience was the nonsensical element of it – the house as big as the moon, the sun in the midst of night. Alternatively, some readers will enjoy creating meaning of a surreal kind, conjuring up in their minds vivid images such as the peacock with the fiery tail, or the eyes in a flame of fire. Or the poem can be read in yet another way:

I saw a peacock.
With a fiery tail I saw a blazing comet.
Drop down hail I saw a Cloud.
With ivy circled round I saw a sturdy Oak.

Although the syntax is a bit peculiar, read like this the poem makes literal sense and some readers will get pleasure from having 'broken the code'.

Meanings beyond the literal

Unlocking the meaning in stories and in poems frequently depends on considering the writer's use of figurative language. We will say more about this in Chapter 8. Some readers struggle to get enjoyment from exploring the significance of metaphors and similes. We have all met very literally minded readers such as the boy whose class had shared a poem about a river that was sad because a man had drowned in its waters. 'Rivers', he said to the teacher witheringly, 'don't talk'.

Uncovering layers of meaning

All primary teachers want to enlarge their pupils' reading repertoires. In recent years we have had the good sense to offer children a wider choice of texts and to encourage them to bring texts of their own choosing into the classroom. Readers, as we have pointed out already, will approach the same text differently at different times in their lives. The door labelled 'poetry' or 'fiction' is not necessarily going to slam shut for ever. It is very important to offer even young readers quality texts whose meanings can be unpeeled like the layers of an onion. It may take years to realise what layers are in the text, and yet we believe that some of that subtlety of meaning will be apparent even to a relatively inexperienced reader. Reading scheme books are excellent for developing reading strategies and skills, but very rarely do they offer these 'layers' that so richly reward continual re-reading, pondering and discussion.

Yet it must not be a case of 'practise on the scheme texts now and then later on you'll be able to tackle some more interesting ones'. Reading is a very difficult business and young readers must be convinced that the game is worth the candle. The texts we offer them from the start must be fun, wacky, engrossing, intriguing and scary, endlessly challenging our ways of looking at life.

Quality in fictional texts

What counts as quality in fiction texts is a matter of subjective judgement to some extent. We very much meant what we said in Chapter 1 about developing your own enthusiasms and tastes as readers. To develop tastes and preferences means also developing a feel for the way certain authors do things. We will risk offering at least an example here of what we mean by quality – what to us 'layers of meaning' might refer to – though one example doesn't make a definition!

We want to talk about a picture book that features very frequently in discussions of children's literature, though we have no regrets about mentioning it yet again. It is *Where the Wild Things Are* by Maurice Sendak (2000). The book opens with Max, the hero of the story, dressed in his wolf suit, and 'making mischief of one kind or another'. As a result, his mother calls him 'WILD THING' and sends him to his room without any supper. The reader is shown, rather than told, some of the kinds of mischief he got up to. This has the advantage of instantly involving the reader in the 'onion peeling' kinds of reading we referred to earlier. We have choices as readers: we can go on to find out what happened next; we can become involved in thinking about our reactions to what Max did that annoyed his mother so much; or we might want to think or talk about how we feel about his punishment.

What happens next is certainly very interesting. 'That very night in Max's room a forest grew and grew until his ceiling was hung with vines and the walls became the world all around . . .' There are rich opportunities here for reading between the lines. Some readers will bring previous experience to bear of escaping from reality into a world of their own creation. Some may be reminded of other texts that they have read like this one. On a first reading, many will not want to pause at all at this point, but will want to find out more about the story. The high point comes when Max arrives at the 'place where the wild things are', and we follow his progress in building a relationship with them. A literal reading enables us to react with a shiver of horror at their 'terrible roars', their 'terrible teeth' and their 'terrible claws'. Or readers might choose to find them funny, or even cuddly. Max is certainly not fazed by them. He becomes their king and they recognise him as 'the most wild thing of all'. He is in charge, and is able to order them off to bed without any supper.

Just when he seems all set for a life of endless 'wild rumpuses' we are told that 'from far away across the world he smelled good things to eat' and so decides to give up being king of where the wild things are. The wild things are not pleased and beg him to stay. They even threaten to eat him, but Max is not at all put out by their threats. He steps into his private boat and sails back into 'the night of his very own room', where he finds his supper waiting for him. Some of the most interesting opportunities for exploring beneath the surface of the text come in discussing (or enacting) what life would have been like with the wild things. Could Max have gone on for ever? Why did he decide not to? It may take many readings, even many years, before children can explore all the links and layers that the book makes possible.

We can compare this text with one that seems similar in some ways: *Row Your Boat*, a traditional rhyming text. There is a version of it by Pippa Goodhart, with illustrations by Stephen Lambert (2007). Two children find themselves, like Max, sailing away in a boat, but here we are told rather than shown that 'life is but a dream', and so we have not really engaged the deeper levels of our own 'meaning-making apparatus' as readers when we arrive at the dreamland the writer has created. It is difficult to read in any other way but literally about the elephants, monkeys, snakes and spiders who await the children's arrival. There is none of the delicious ambiguity of Sendak's creations. In his book we see Max befriending the creatures, even becoming their king, and yet, and yet . . . they are still 'terrible', the writer reminds us, and do actually threaten to eat him. We as readers must decide how we are going to interpret this. In *Row Your Boat*, when the lion roars, there is no ambiguity at all. The children very wisely decide to run back to the boat

> Before the lion catches us
> And eats us for his tea!

There is nothing wrong with this text; it is delightful in many ways. The words are set to music and the children will very much enjoy singing them. But it does not have the quality of Sendak's text in the sense that it will not repay many re-readings, because most of its meaning resides on a literal level. It asks very much less of its readers.

In this chapter and the last we have given a fairly brief overview of some of the issues involved in writing and reading texts. In Chapters 9, 10, 11 and 12 we will take some of these points further by looking at specific examples of fiction and non-fiction texts. Texts depend of course on arrangements of words to create their effects, and it is to the variety of ways of arranging them that we will turn next.

Summary

In this chapter we have discussed:

- reading as an active, meaning-making process;

- the range of purposes for which we read and the kinds of reading behaviours that are needed to fulfil those purposes;

- the layers of meaning that can be uncovered in some quality texts, repaying many re-readings and reinterpretations.

Activity 2: Audit your text-level knowledge

1. Please read the following extract carefully. The questions we are asking you to think about are to help you consider your own knowledge about texts and are not necessarily in the form you would use if you were raising these issues with children.

> What were Dinosaurs?
>
> What would it have been like to have lived when dinosaurs ruled the earth? No book can really show you. You have to use your imagination. Imagine the ground shaking under your feet as a herd of 10,000 Triceratops stampedes towards you. Imagine the sound of a five-tonne duckbill dinosaur calling to his mate with its long, trombone-like head crest. Imagine the sight and smell of a herd of 10 tonne Brachiosaurus in a conifer forest, pine needles showering down from their munching mouths, 14 metres above you. Dinosaurs lived millions of years ago, long before humans existed. Scientists who studied the fossil bones of dinosaurs thought they must have been giant, cold-blooded reptiles. They saw them as slow-moving, stupid 'mistakes' which died out to make room for the superior mammals. Recent discoveries have shattered this view. We now know that dinosaurs were a great success.
>
> (Theodorou 1995: 4)

   (a) How would you sum up the author's main purpose in writing this text? At what point in your reading does this become apparent? If you had the book in front of you, do you think there would be other indications of the purpose of the text?
   (b) Do you think the author had particular readers in mind? What evidence would you draw on?
   (c) In terms of its structure and syntax, the piece falls into two roughly equal parts. At what point in the text would you say the second part begins?
   (d) How would you describe, in general terms, what the author is trying to do in the first part of the text? In the second part?
   (e) From what you have said so far about the text, what categories of content do you predict will be found in some of the book's eight chapters?
   (f) As well as chapter headings, what do you think the book will contain that will help readers to access the material successfully?

2. Identifying text types. Research has shown that there are six non-fiction types of text that occur very frequently in everyday life (see p. 38). It therefore would probably be helpful to children to introduce them to examples of each of these and to support them in creating their own. To help you to think about some of the characteristics of these text types, see if you can match each of the opening lines below to its appropriate label. They are jumbled up at present. Think carefully in each case about the evidence you are drawing on.

(a)   Make a nose using papier-mâché, paint or sticky paper, a   Novel
      piece of an egg box, a bottle cork or a button.

(b)   When the cocoa beans are dry, they are packed into sacks   Personal
      and taken to the buying station.   recount

(c)   Now then, I was twelve, rising thirteen, when our Daniel got   Persuasive
      killed. Aye . . . it was a long time ago. I'm talking about a   piece
      time of day eighty-three years back. Eighty-three years. It's a
      time of day that's past your imagining.

(d)   In my opinion, school uniform should be abolished.   Poem

(e)   The wind was a torrent of darkness among the gusty trees,   Explanation
      The moon was a ghostly galleon, tossed upon cloudy seas.

(f)   Our class enjoyed our trip to Chester Zoo and we would like   Instructions
      to go again.

See pages 162–4 for a commentary on this activity.

6

What big teeth you have, grammar!

We chose this title for Chapter 6 because many people seem to be afraid of grammar, seeing it as a set of rules waiting to catch them out. We want to persuade you that grammar should rather be seen as a resource, serving writers' and speakers' purposes as they struggle to express meanings in the texts they are creating. The next two chapters will not turn you into an expert on English grammar, but we hope that they will at least begin to make clear what a knowledge of grammar has to offer to primary teachers and therefore to the children in their classes.

What is grammar?

It is possible but fairly unusual to find texts that consist of one or two words only. There are examples, spoken or written, such as:

- Help!
- Nice day!
- No entry.

These sentences, known as minor sentences, don't obey the usual rules of text construction. For more information on minor sentences, see Crystal (2004a: 34). Lists are another example of texts that can consist of words in groups or in isolation; perhaps one reason why they are a popular text type among young writers is because the writer is free from the constraints of the rules of syntax.

Syntax

'Syntax' is the term used for the set of rules governing the ways in which words are regularly combined into clauses appropriate for a particular text, including rules for word order and word endings (inflections). It is possible to invent a sentence that obeys the rules of syntax but which is perfectly meaningless, as in:

- Siv grockles lubed transomly.

Though you have never seen these words before, it is possible to deduce from the word order and endings such as 'ed' and 'ly' what work each of these words is doing, though you can have little or no idea of the semantics, or meaning, of the sentence. To understand a little more about semantic processing, or how we make meaning from what we hear or read, think about a sentence such as:

- Dogs must be carried on the Underground.

Unless they can process the meaning of this correctly, all those who have left Fido at home will be heading for the bus stop.

Inflectional endings

The term 'inflection' refers to the ways in which words change their spellings, or acquire extra bits at the beginning or the end, depending on the work the words do in a sentence (for example he runs, he is running, he ran). The parts added on are known as prefixes if they are attached to the beginning of a root word, and suffixes if they are added on at the end.

How words work within sentences

Grammar also provides a description of how words can function in different ways in sentences, depending on their place in the sentence and their relationship with other words. For example, in the sentence 'I grow beetroot in my allotment' the word 'beetroot' is functioning as a noun, but in the sentence 'Beetroot sandwiches were Fred's favourites' the word 'beetroot' is being used as an adjective, to describe 'sandwiches'. It might be possible to invent a sentence in which 'beetroot' becomes a verb:

'What did you do for lunch today?'
'Oh, today I beetrooted, and I shall courgette tomorrow.'

A fuller definition of these word classes – 'noun', 'verb' and 'adjective' – can be found later in this chapter.

Is it really necessary to teach grammar?

It's clear that the study of grammar disappeared from the curricula of some schools to such an extent that many people have been left with a feeling of complete ignorance about it. Now, primary teachers are expected to have a fairly detailed knowledge. One of the most difficult questions to give a clear answer to, though we are sure you are hoping for one, is 'Is it necessary to provide children with specific grammar teaching?' Many times recently we have heard people say, 'I've lived for thirty [or forty or fifty] years without knowing what a conjunction was, and it hasn't done me any harm! Why should I teach it to children?' One of the most difficult but most important tasks for primary teachers is to ensure that they pass on knowledge of grammar to children in such a way that it helps to make the children more discriminating readers, writers and speakers and empowers them to produce written and spoken texts that both embody what it is they want to say and make a suitable impact on those listening or reading.

What does it mean to be knowledgeable about grammar?

Just because some people can't state explicitly what a conjunction is certainly does not mean that they are unable to express themselves adequately in speech or in writing. One of the most important distinctions to be clear about as you acquire more knowledge about language is the difference between implicit and explicit language knowledge. We have described in previous chapters how we learn the processes involved in putting language together, as people who are actively participating in carrying out a range of language jobs or functions in a society. We have spoken of the kinds of feedback we all receive that enable us to fine-tune our utterances so that we accomplish our purposes and satisfy the needs of those we are communicating with. When some people express an ignorance or fear of the rules of grammar, they may mean that they cannot put these rules into words, can't explain what a conjunction is, or identify a subordinate clause in a sentence, though their speech and writing will be full of conjunctions, prepositions and subordinate clauses.

Finding the right context for grammar teaching

If you are one of those who have doubts about the value of grammar teaching, we think it is certainly worth considering whether a certain amount of grammatical knowledge, provided it is taught in context, supports and extends children's implicit use of language. This may be especially true for those children we referred to earlier who do not pick up a variety of sentence patterns simply from being exposed to them as readers and speakers, but who might be able to bring more variety to the texts they create, and more sensitivity to other writers' and speakers' achievements, if they had more explicit teaching.

Standard English and regional varieties

There are almost certainly some people whose dislike of grammar is connected with a sense of inadequacy about their powers as language users. One might have hoped that many years of free state education would have eradicated people's feelings of inadequacy, but this seems to be not entirely the case. If you look on the website of the Practical English Programme, you will find that their 'New Course in Practical English' promises higher earnings, the ability to control every situation, greater popularity and a more active social life!

How can standard English be defined?

Linguists, unlike purveyors of English programmes, might argue with the notion of there being one 'correct' form of English grammar. Linguists recognise that there is more than one grammar of English; for example, each variety of regional English has a grammar, a set of rules understood and practised by the users of the dialect, though the rules are not written down. It is true that there is one form of English, referred to as 'standard English', which is perceived as having higher status than the others. Standard English has been defined as

> that variety of English which is usually used in print and which is normally taught in schools and to non-native speakers using the language. It is also the variety which is normally spoken by educated people and used in news broadcasts and other similar situations.
>
> (LINC 1992: 355)

It is likely that those people who feel uneasy about their own language are aware that there are some usages in their spoken, if not in their written, English that deviate from what is regarded as 'standard English'. Non-standard varieties of English, or regional dialects, are characterised by grammatical features and vocabulary that are typical of a particular geographical area. Standard English is also regarded by linguists such as David Crystal (2004a: 12–15) as a dialect, but not a regional one. It is associated with upper- and middle-class social groups particularly, but it affects everyone because of its official status and widespread use, especially in the written form.

Varieties of standard English

Standard English itself takes a variety of forms, with standard American English being different from standard Scottish English and standard Australian English. The variants of standard English, like all forms of language, are constantly changing and evolving. Though syntactic patterns don't change very rapidly, vocabulary is always being added or, in the case of words such as 'frock' or 'wireless', is disappearing from use. There is more to linguistic change than just vocabulary, however. Styles of speaking and writing, the usages people consider appropriate for any text they find themselves constructing, are to some extent like styles of dressing or home decorating. They change much more rapidly than one might think. Here, for example, is Rollo Spencer, an upper-class, successful, city businessman, in *The Weather in the Streets*, written in 1936 by Rosamund Lehmann. He is expressing his concern to the book's heroine, Olivia, on hearing that her father is very ill:

> I say, I'm most terribly sorry. Why didn't you tell me? How awful for you . . . I do hope you'll find it isn't so bad . . . I expect he'll be all right, honestly I do. Daddy was most frightfully ill last winter – heart and kidneys and God knows what – all the works. They said he'd never be able to shoot or fish again, and have to live in an armchair, if he ever left his bed again – and now you should see him. He's as right as rain – practically . . . Do give him my love if he remembers me . . . I do wish there was something I could do . . . Might I ring up? Would it be a bore?
>
> (Lehmann 1936: 21)

We must confess that upper-class city businessmen are not a group of people with whom we frequently find ourselves engaged in creating a text of any kind, but we find it hard to imagine that the sympathy would be expressed in quite the same terms today.

As a general principle, fluidity and change in language are to be welcomed rather than feared or disapproved of, as a sign of lively minds constantly seeking new ways to express themselves. From time to time of course each of us may cringe at some aspect of language use that offends us, but this should not send us harking nostalgically back to some non-existent golden age of English.

A dialect continuum

The influence of the mass media – offering everyone the opportunity to hear and read a variety of forms of English – and increased job mobility are two of the factors that explain why many people today operate on a dialect continuum, choosing and assembling their words according to whom they are speaking to, where and for what purpose. Even when speakers are at what might be thought of as 'the dialect end' of their personal speech continuum, it would be a mistake to think that in this day and age the grammar or vocabulary they use will be very different from the grammar of standard English. A few years ago, an old man who lived in Huddersfield, in West Yorkshire, told a colleague of ours:

> Well, I remember this fellow telling me that his grandfather told him that in his day, you could tell a Holmfirth man from a Honley man, a Honley man from, say, Lockwood or Berry Brow and Huddersfield – all the way down the valley the dialect differed. You know, there was a subtle difference, and I remember George and I were producing a sort of pageant over at Slaithwaite and . . . they didn't know what 'laiking' was over there. The young people said, 'Well, – what's laiking?' What do you mean when you say 'laiking'? It's an old dialect word for 'play' isn't it?

You might find it interesting to try to collect some examples of dialect usage from your own area, though you may have to ask older members of the community, particularly for examples of vocabulary.

- In West Yorkshire, for example, it might still be possible to find someone who has just got off a crowded bus who might say 'We were fair thrussen up' (crowded together).
- Forms of the second person singular pronouns 'thee' and 'thou' can still be heard in Barnsley, in South Yorkshire, as in 'What does tha mean by that?'
- Non-standard uses of the verb 'to be' are fairly widespread in parts of the north: 'I were waiting two hours for a bus this morning!'
- In some parts of Lancashire, it is common for people to use a non-standard past participle for 'to sit' and 'to stand': 'I was sat [or 'were sat'] watching the film' or 'I was stood at the window.'

- Other non-standard usages that have survived include the double negative frequently heard in south London, amongst other places: 'I don't know nothing about that.'

The examples we have given here come from our own first-hand experience, as we have moved around the British Isles because of education or jobs. You can find a more systematic account of surviving examples of regional grammars in Trudgill *et al.* (2005). Again, let us stress that there is a lot of common ground with regard to both grammar and vocabulary that all dialects share, though some dialects seem to have retained more distinctive features than others.

Accent

It is important to be clear that dialect, which refers to varieties of grammar and vocabulary, is not the same thing as accent. Accent refers to the ways in which speakers pronounce the sounds of English. Someone with a Lancashire accent, for example, will probably make no distinction between the /oo/ sounds in 'cook' and 'moon'. The 'a' in 'path' may sound like the 'a' in 'man'. It is perfectly possible to speak standard English with a regional accent.

Received pronunciation

Just as standard English is a high-prestige variant – and usage of it tends to be associated, in many people's minds, with power and status – so there is an accent, received pronunciation, which has no regional connotations, and is associated with, for example, BBC newsreaders or television commentators on grand state occasions. It's possible that some readers may consider this accent 'posh' or 'plummy'. Whereas it would generally be considered advisable to try to use standard English when attending a job interview, to use received pronunciation runs some risk of attracting a hostile, 'Who does she think she is?' reception. The number of people who speak received pronunciation or something close to it is much smaller than the number of speakers and writers of standard English.

Accent as an emotive issue

Reactions to accent are another fascinating area for further study, should you have the opportunity. You will be aware of how producers of television commercials are adept at choosing a suitable accent to sell their products – rural accents, such as those of Dorset or Somerset, to sell 'wholesome' products, such as brown bread; French accents for expensive perfumes; German or Japanese accents to sell cars! Attitudes and prejudices towards accents are quite illogical but often firmly entrenched, with rural accents tending to condemn their owners to being seen as slow (but trustworthy) or urban accents being labelled 'ugly'. It is not unusual for those of our students who have Liverpool accents to find themselves labelled 'football hooligans', though they may never have been within half a mile of Anfield . . . or Goodison Park! This is one example of the responses we have learned to associate with the accents; they have nothing to do with the quality of the sounds that come out of the speakers' mouths, much less with the characteristics of those who utter them.

Substandard forms of English

You need to be aware that the term 'non-standard', which we have used to describe regional varieties of English, is sometimes applied to language that has no particular roots in history, as dialects have, but which results from carelessness, as for example when people say 'I'll have one of them books', or write 'I should of done it years ago.' The term 'non-standard' is then being used as a polite variant of 'substandard'. Slang also lies outside the standard/non-standard dichotomy. Standard English speakers use slang, and regions have slang terms familiar to those who live there. The term refers to expressions that come and go very quickly, more often used in speech than in writing. They tend to indicate that their speakers belong to various groups, possibly age groups, social groups or groups who spend a lot of time together in shared activities. One of the features that most obviously dates Rollo Spencer in the book we quoted earlier is his use of slang expressions: 'Daddy was most frightfully ill . . . He's as right as rain . . .' To be still using these expressions today almost certainly marks one out as being over 40.

The rest of what we have to say in this chapter refers to the spoken and written language systems of standard English.

The grammars of speech and of writing are not identical

Some characteristics of speech

The grammars of speech and of writing are by no means identical, though obviously there are large areas of overlap. If speech is planned and rehearsed, it frequently takes on more of the characteristics of writing. Spontaneous speech, on the other hand, is put together too quickly for very much consideration to be given to syntactical choices.

Ellipsis

Frequently, when speakers are talking quickly and spontaneously, some parts of the sentence are omitted:

- Want some?
- I'd like to help you but I can't.

It would be a mistake to think of these as being examples of how speech is 'sloppy' or 'more careless' than writing. In some contexts, it would make one sound very odd, even unfriendly, to say 'Would you like some tea?', though there may be formal contexts in which a speaker would choose that option. It's frequently the case that speakers don't use whole sentences when the context is an informal one. In these cases the 'units of language' that go to make up the text are known as 'utterances'. In the second example above, which is a sentence, though an incomplete one, the meaning of the second half of the sentence is quite clear by referring back to the first half. This looking back to find the meaning is called 'anaphoric reference'. It would make a text sound very tedious, indeed rather ridiculous, if everything were always stated in full: 'I'd like to help you but I can't help you'. In grammatical description, this shortening of sentences is referred to as 'ellipsis'. Elided forms of words also frequently occur in speech, such as 'I'd' and 'can't' in the second example. 'Elision' is the term that refers to the omission of sounds in connected speech.

False starts

False starts are common in spontaneous speech, as the speaker realises that an utterance or a sentence is going in the wrong direction.

- We thought we might, well, would it be a good idea to . . .

The 'well' signals in this case that a change of direction is coming. It gives the speaker a fractional bit of thinking time.

Another way of changing direction, common in some speech contexts but not acceptable in writing, is in a sentence like the following:

- You know that girl who used to live next door, I saw her in the supermarket.

Fillers

There are other 'words' or sounds that provide speakers with a bit of time to think, like 'um' and 'er'. We've spoken about the speed with which a spontaneous text is built up, with several people taking turns. An additional advantage of fillers is that they enable a speaker to hang on to their turn, to refuse to relinquish the conversational ball, so to speak.

Writing, as we pointed out in the text chapter, can sometimes be dashed off in a way that makes it sound very like spontaneous speech. Some children tend to cling to forms of written syntax that are not very different from those of speech. If grammar is to be taught successfully in primary schools, one of the goals must be to enable children to feel confident to produce a wider range of sentence patterns, including the more literary ones that would sound most peculiar being uttered by someone standing at a bus stop. It would be unusual, for example, for a speaker, at least in ordinary conversation, to use this style of sentence construction:

Long ago when the world was brand new, before animals or birds, the sun rose into the sky and brought the first day.

(Hughes 1971: 9)

Putting sentences together

What is involved in constructing a sentence? Sentences are much more difficult to define than we sometimes lead children to believe. It's easy to describe one as 'beginning with a capital letter and ending with a full stop', but this gives little or no help with the difficult question of what comes in between these two.

Sentences, whether spoken or written, fulfil four functions. They can be used:

- to make statements;
- to ask questions;
- to utter exclamations;
- to give instructions (or these might be expressed more strongly as orders or commands).

All of these can be either positive or negative.

Sentences are classified into three types: simple, compound and complex. Experienced writers and speakers will try to match the type of sentence to the meanings they are trying to express.

Simple sentences

The word 'simple' is not used in grammar with a meaning akin to 'unsophisticated', nor does it imply anything about the length of the sentence. It is a technical term meaning that the sentence contains only one of each of the basic sentence requirements:

- a subject (someone or something the speaker or writer wants to focus on);
- some kind of activity associated with the subject (though the activity might be a mental activity such as 'being' or 'thinking').

Speculations on the origins of sentences

No one knows for sure how language began, but it is tempting to imagine some of our early ancestors using their emergent language skills to label significant aspects of their environment, such as 'Lion!' This is not of much use, however, unless you can tell people what the lion is doing: 'The lion is coming!' or 'The lion is eating Ashok!'

Types of sentence

These examples represent two very common sentence types:

- The first consists of a subject ('the lion') and a part of the verb 'to come' ('is coming'). Though not particularly informative, the sentence is grammatically complete.
- The second sentence has another element: there is a subject ('the lion' again), an activity ('is eating') and this time something that is being eaten (the unfortunate 'Ashok'). This last element in the sentence is called the direct object. The direct object is the person or thing on the receiving end of the activity.

Verbs are the class of words used to say what the activity in the sentence is: those followed by a direct object are called transitive verbs and the others are intransitive.

SVO (subject/verb/object) sentences

It's quite unusual to find very short sentences with only a subject (not described at all), a verb and an object (again with no information about it). Even in the speech of young children, more words are woven in, giving extra information. One place where these minimal sentences are frequently found is in the early levels of reading schemes, and, because it's rare to find these sentence structures in everyday life, this gives those texts their rather odd sound. Here is an example from the Ginn reading scheme, 'All Aboard', but almost all reading schemes will use the same minimalist sentence structures in the early levels. *The Parrot*, a stage one introductory text, has a series of statements with the same subject each time, 'Sam', the same verb, 'saw', and a series of direct objects.

- Sam saw a parrot.
- Sam saw a flag.
- Sam saw a sword.
- Sam saw a hat.
- Sam saw a pirate.
- Sam saw Rosie.

In *Jabeen and the New Moon* in the same scheme, Jabeen remains the subject throughout, though you will notice that she is referred to as 'she' after the first page. 'Saw' is the verb again, until we get to the last page, but as before we have a variety of direct objects.

- Jabeen saw her new kameez.
- She saw her new shalwar.
- She saw her new sandals.
- She saw her new bangles.
- She saw the new moon.
- She put on her new clothes!

Though the text still sounds odd, judged in terms of 'real' text such as we might find in everyday life, just the shift from 'Jabeen' to 'she' helps to make it sound a little bit more natural. The writer's prime purpose in writing the text in this rather monotonous way is presumably to emphasise the subject/verb/direct object sentence pattern for readers who are still at an early stage in understanding sentence structure.

SVC (subject/verb/complement) sentences

If the activity in the sentence is represented by part of the verb 'to be' the situation is rather different.

- Rosie is Sam's sister.

- Nog is our dog.

- Tomorrow might be warm and sunny.

- She was the director.

Here, 'Rosie' and 'Sam's sister' are different ways of naming the same object. 'Nog' and 'our dog' are one and the same. In the last two sentences a 'state of being' is described rather than an activity. In sentences like these four, the words that come after any part of the verb 'to be' are described not as the direct object but the complement. This is not a complete description of the complement element in a sentence.

The building blocks of sentences

Nouns

What kinds or 'classes' of words can do the job of being the subject, the object or the complement in a sentence? Very often this function is fulfilled by words behaving as nouns. Nouns are the words used by speakers and writers to name people, things, actions and ideas. Nouns can be grouped into two divisions: proper and common. Common nouns can be 'count' or 'non-count' types, and both of these types can provide concrete or abstract examples. A proper noun is the name of a specific person or a place or perhaps a special time such as 'Easter'. Proper nouns are written with initial capital letters. 'Jabeen' is an example of a proper noun, as are 'Sam' and 'Rosie'. Count nouns refer to individual items such as parrots, or swords, or shalwars. Non-count nouns refer to an undifferentiated mass, such as sunshine. An abstract noun is something you can't see or touch, such as 'courage', 'anger' or 'loyalty'. Because we are quoting from books for beginner readers, these passages contain no abstract nouns.

Pronouns

We have seen how odd it sounds in *The Parrot* to mention Sam time and time again. In *Jabeen and the New Moon* 'Jabeen' was quickly replaced by 'she'. These are examples of a class of words called pronouns, which, as the name suggests, can work 'on behalf of' nouns. Pronouns are a large and quite complex class of words. Very often, the ones that stand in as the subject or object of a sentence are a subgroup called personal pronouns. They are used more frequently than any other types of pronoun.

Pronouns 'in the first person' allow the speaker(s) or writer(s) to include themselves in what is being said:

- I, me, myself;

- we, us, ourselves.

The sentence 'We like dressing up as pirates' is written in the first person plural.

If a writer or speaker wants to address someone directly, it's possible to use a pronoun 'in the second person'. Second person pronouns include 'you' and 'yourselves'. An example of a sentence using a second person pronoun is: 'Do you like dressing up?' This direct address to the reader is frequently employed in books for young children.

The third person allows speakers or writers to refer to things apart from themselves or the person(s) being addressed:

- he, him, himself;
- she, her, herself, it, itself;
- they, them, themselves.

It must be clear to readers to whom the 'he', 'she', 'they' or 'it' refers. Usually, the noun to which the pronoun refers has been mentioned earlier in the text: 'Jabeen saw her new kameez. She saw her new shalwar. She saw her new sandals.' We know that the 'she' in the second and third sentences is the same person as 'Jabeen' in the first sentence.

Adjectives

Most listeners or readers are greedy for information, and usually like to know more about the subject or the object, or more about the action that is being carried out. In *Jabeen and the New Moon* 'her' and 'new' are the words that give us more information about the kameez, the shalwar, the sandals, the bangles, the moon and the clothes. They are adjectives. They can help to make the text more precise, for example when they give

- numbers or amounts of things: three, several, many, lots;
- the colour: red, vivid, rainbow-hued;
- the feel: fluffy, smooth, hard-edged.

But they are dangerous things. Include too many of them and a text can quickly sound cluttered and overwritten. We urged you in the text chapter to see reading as an interactive process, with the readers doing a lot of the work of meaning making by bringing their own ideas and associations to bear. Too many adjectives can make this difficult, constraining readers from making a personal response. Children should be advised to use this class of words sparingly and thoughtfully.

The definite and indefinite article

On the front cover of *The Parrot*, the first word, 'the', is an example of the definite article. To use it with 'parrot' indicates that the writer wants us to think of a specific parrot, a particular one. She is not going to write about parrots in general. It would be important then, with young readers, for teachers to spend time discussing the title page. Here we have *The Parrot* again, and now something hinted at on the front cover is more clearly discernible: the parrot is attached to a stick and is being held in someone's hand. We, the readers, are now in possession of some important information, which is reinforced by the first page of the story proper. This page is a little bit confusing because it seems to show four parrots on sticks. Most children would need help with understanding the text convention here. The picture does not actually show four parrots but 'the' parrot being wiggled about. Sam, the main character in the story, does not have the knowledge that we, the readers, have. On the second page of the story, we see the parrot, but the hand and the stick are hidden by a fence. And we are told that 'Sam saw "a" parrot'. 'A' is the indefinite article and its use usually indicates that the noun has not been mentioned already. The fact that we know it has puts us in a very special position. It is only at the end of the story that Sam finds out what we knew from the beginning, that 'the' parrot, the one in the title, the only one the author is concerned about, belongs to Rosie, as do all the other pirate trappings that Sam has caught glimpses of.

The last sentence is 'Sam saw Rosie.' We have an example of 'zero articles' here. We would only put 'a' or 'the' with proper nouns in very special circumstances, as in:

'I saw Rosie.'
'Do you mean the Rosie who is Sam's sister?'
'No, not that Rosie, the Rosie who is in our class.'

Articles in generalising statements

One of the important things about certain types of non-fiction writing, such as reports, is that they frequently deal with a class of things in general, rather than named examples. It's possible then that such a piece would have zero articles in the title, which might be 'Whales', for example. The writer might then go on perhaps to use the indefinite article: 'A whale eats . . .', 'A whale lives . . .', though 'the whale' could alternatively be used, not in the sense of one whale, called Willy, but referring to the whole class of these creatures: 'The whale is a fascinating mammal . . .'

Adverbs

We have mentioned already that not all verbs take a direct object. Those that do not are called 'intransitive' verbs. Here is an intransitive verb at work, still from the introductory level of the Ginn reading scheme 'All Aboard'. It's in a story called *Grandad's Balloon*.

Grandad's balloon went up.
Rosie's balloon went up.
Tilak's balloon went up.
Mo's balloon went up.
Grandad's balloon went . . .
POP!

We come here to an example (although a relatively simple one) of why people find grammar irritating and difficult. At first sight it might seem as if the pattern of these sentences is very similar to what we have looked at already (see Figure 6.1).

Word order is very important in English sentences, and children become aware of this very quickly. Even when they are only at the stage of putting two words together, English-speaking children always put them in the right order: 'Biccy gone', not 'Gone biccy'. They develop a feel for what I have listed in Figure 6.1 as 'column one' words,

Sam	saw	a parrot.
Jabeen	saw	her new kameez.
Tilak's balloon	went	up.
Grandad's balloon	went	POP!

FIGURE 6.1 Word order in English sentences.

'column two' words and 'column three' words. Even when putting much longer sentences together, it is seldom the word order that we find difficult. The problem is not with instinctively sorting the words out into the right order, but with having an explicit understanding of the variety of words that can occupy the third column.

If the word in the third column is a direct object, it answers the question 'What?' 'Sam saw what?' 'Jabeen saw what?' We can turn the sentence round and write it another way: 'The parrot was seen by Sam', 'The new kameez was seen by Jabeen'. In the third sentence, 'up' doesn't answer the question 'What?', but 'Where?' Actually we have a difficulty with this sentence because the subject is a balloon. Especially in the last sentence, when grandad's balloon went 'pop' it might seem to many children that 'pop' is answering the question 'What?' It's actually answering the question 'How did it go?' Another way of thinking about the difference between the third column in these last two sentences is to understand that they can't be transformed as the first two can. We can't say 'Up was gone by Tilak's balloon' or 'POP was gone by grandad's balloon'. 'To go' is an intransitive verb and it is therefore not followed by a direct object. 'Up' is an adverb of place, telling us where the balloon went, and 'pop' is an adverb of manner, telling us how the balloon met its end. Adverbs, in other words, give us more information about the activity in the sentence; the traditional way of putting this is to say that they 'modify' (rather than 'describe') the verb.

Kinds of adverb

Other types of adverb you will meet frequently are adverbs of time, such as 'yesterday' or 'later', and adverbs of reason, which, as you would expect, tell us why something happened. It usually takes more than one word to give a reason for something, as in 'because I say so . . .', and so we will say more about adverbs of reason when we come to phrases and clauses.

Adverbs can move about a bit!

Though we have had examples here of adverbs in the 'column three' position, they can move about in sentences depending on the emphasis that the writer wants to give. It would have been possible to write 'Up went Tilak's balloon' or 'POP! went grandad's balloon'. Writers of the early stages of reading schemes frequently seem to make an effort to keep the syntactic shape of the sentences as close as possible to that of everyday speech. All readers are helped if they can bring some previous experience to bear when they are reading. For beginner readers, their previous language experience can be drawn only either from speech or from what they have had read to them. 'Up went Tilak's balloon' is less likely to occur in everyday speech than the form in which the sentence was actually written.

Story syntax

Although it is helpful to have everyday sentence shapes reinforced when children begin to read, it would be unfortunate if they did not also hear and participate in the reading of texts with more varied, more literary syntax. It is sometimes all too easy to hear the relentless rhythms of 'reading scheme syntax' in some young children's writing. These are children who may have been denied the variety of sentence shapes that can be found in texts like Ted Hughes' (1963) *How the Whale Became*, which we quoted earlier. They need to be constantly reminded of the fact that grammar is not there to constrain language users, but to be adapted to their purposes.

In the opening sentence of *The Time of the Lion* (1999), Caroline Pitcher writes: 'One day while his village slept, Joseph heard a ROAR thunderclap across the wide savannah.' 'Thunderclap' is usually used as a noun, but here the writer has decided to make it a verb, with very dramatic effect. Children should be offered a rich diet of poetry and prose from writers who are not afraid to innovate and experiment, so that they can quickly come to appreciate and try out for themselves the variety of grammatical choices that are possible in English.

Verbs

Verbs are such a large and complex word class that we have decided to give them a section to themselves. Of all the words in a sentence, the nouns and the verbs are the most vital parts. Let us go back for a moment to Ashok and his friends in their cave, threatened by that lion. It would be helpful to know whether the lion was coming quickly or slowly; it might be reassuring to know that it was an old lion or a toothless lion; it would be interesting to know if it was morning or evening when the lion came. When all is said and done, however, the two vital bits of information are (1) that there was a lion and (2) that it was coming towards the cave, particularly as we saw this text as a speech being addressed to Ashok himself, and not as part of a sad tale told round the camp fire to frighten the little ones for years afterwards.

The infinitive

When listing verbs, to learn them in a foreign language for example, we usually find them in their infinitive or 'base' form, the form that starts with 'to': to eat, to sleep, to walk, to climb, to run, to skip, to look and so on. The word 'infinitive' implies having no ends or boundaries. The rules of English syntax on the other hand require that all sentences must have a finite form of a verb in them. Where do the boundaries come from to make the infinitive finite? The first boundary is concerned with something you have met already: the concept of 'person'.

Person

FIRST PERSON

In describing pronouns earlier in this chapter we referred to the fact that writers and speakers can structure their texts in such a way that they are describing their own actions.

- I eat cornflakes for breakfast.
- I slept till late this morning.
- I was walking along the road when I saw my friend.

This is writing or speaking in the first person and it gives a personal slant to the text. Of course, it may be the writer or speaker and someone else who is doing these things, in which case we would have 'we' and the verb in the first person plural. Subject and verb must agree as to person (first, second or third) and number (singular or plural) in standard English, though sentences such as 'I were hoping for a new job', with a singular subject but a plural verb, are heard in some dialects.

SECOND PERSON

Speakers frequently, and writers quite often, want to address their listeners or readers directly, and so they will write in the second person: 'You said that you would help me.' Standard English makes no distinction between the second person singular and the second person plural, with regard either to the pronoun or to the form of the verb, though again in some dialects, and in texts of a certain age, 'thou' will be found for the second person singular, and a verb ending '-est', as in 'Thou makest me glad . . .'

THIRD PERSON

It is frequently felt to be advisable to construct a text in a more impersonal way, mentioning neither oneself nor any particular readers. Then the third person will be used, either singular or plural. This might be a noun or a pronoun, as we have seen already.

When speakers and writers have made their decisions to structure their texts in the first, second or third person, singular or plural, the verb must follow suit. For example, let us suppose a text is being written in the present tense and the verb 'to give' is being used. Texts in the first or second person, whether singular or plural, would have the same form of the verb:

- I give;
- we give;
- you give.

However, in the third person singular, an inflectional ending must be added:

- he gives;
- she gives;
- it gives.

Once speakers or writers have elected to compose texts in the first, second or third person, they must put in place one of the verb 'boundaries' by choosing the appropriate inflectional endings.

Tense

The second important boundary relates to tense. A speaker or writer must decide whether the text is to be in one of the forms of the present tense, or in a past tense. English has no future tense ending, but it has several ways of expressing future time. One way is to use an adverb of time, as in the sentence 'I am going tomorrow'. (For other ways, see also comments on modal verbs below.)

It is generally expected that, once chosen, the tense will be maintained throughout the text, unless there is a good reason to change it. One reason might be to include some direct speech, the actual words spoken by a character in a text. Direct speech, for example within a narrative, might be in the present tense, though the story is being told in the past.

Goldilocks peered in at the window. 'I wonder who lives here', she thought.
Here we have a third person singular subject, Goldilocks, and a past tense of the verb 'to peer'. It is a regular verb and so it forms this past tense by adding the inflection ' ed'. Many English verbs are not regular. We had the verb 'to go' earlier, in the story about the balloon; there is no past form 'goed'. When Goldilocks starts to speak, she of course refers to herself in the first person singular, and the words she speaks are in a present tense, because she is 'wondering' as she is speaking.

Modality

Writers or speakers have one other choice to make with regard to which finite verb form to use – one that helps them to express a judgement about the likelihood of events. They can do this by employing one of a set of verbs called 'modals', of which there are a limited number. Crystal (2004a: 102–3) includes nine verbs in this class, with four more 'marginal modals'. The 'main modals' are 'will', 'would', 'shall', 'should', 'may', 'might', 'can', 'could', 'must'. Teachers and parents often try to instil in children the distinction between 'can' and 'may':

- Can I leave the table please?
- You can, but you may not.

However, 'may' in conversational English is beginning to sound increasingly archaic. 'Can I sit here?' is much more likely to be the modal form chosen by a young person than 'May I?', and so the teacher's comment may not be understood or may at best seem rather carping.

Auxiliaries

It's frequently the case that to complete the tense of the verb they have chosen, speakers or writers must use more than one word:

			stay
		has	stayed
	had	been	staying
must	have	been	staying

A verb, even when it consists of only one word, 'stay' or 'eats' or 'reads' or 'hoped', is described as a verb phrase. This is another of those irritating aspects of grammar because generally it helps to be able to define a phrase to children as 'a group of words acting together'. (There is more discussion of phrases in the next chapter.)

The verbs that sometimes help to make up tenses are known as auxiliary verbs. Parts of the verbs 'to be', 'to have' and 'to do' frequently function as auxiliary verbs. As you can see above, more than one auxiliary can be used at a time.

There are a number of forms of the past and present. Some grammarians call each of these 'tenses', for example the 'perfect tense' and the 'pluperfect tense'. Crystal (2004a: 96–9) calls them 'aspects'. Labelling them all is not something that native speakers are usually taught to do, though you may have met these labels if you have learned another language. We don't think it would be appropriate for children at Key Stage 2 to struggle with this labelling but sometimes children may need help if they are constructing a text in the past tense but something is further back in the text than the rest. 'Cinderella lived with her father and her ugly sisters. She had been a happy child until her mother died when she was three.' Here, the second sentence, using the auxiliary 'had', describes events that are no longer ongoing when the story starts, but are further back in time. To have written 'has been' instead would have implied that the situation was continuing into the time that the story is dealing with, whereas, in fact, this situation is over before the story begins.

'-ed' and '-ing' participles

In some tenses, or 'aspects', alongside the auxiliaries are forms of the verb that, in the case of regular verbs, carry the inflectional endings '-ed' and '-ing'. Examples are:

- has stayed;
- has been staying.

The '-ed' participle acting as part of a verb phrase

'-ed' is an inflectional ending that we have met already, forming a past tense of regular verbs: 'wanted', 'helped', 'climbed' and so on. (It's worth pointing out to children that, although all these are regular past tenses, formed by adding '-ed' to the infinitive form of the verb, they don't all sound the same. We can hear /t/ in 'helped', /d/ in 'climbed' and /ed/ in 'wanted'.)

We are now meeting '-ed' forms in another guise, however, working alongside an auxiliary. If we write 'He has stayed . . .' then the form of the verb 'stayed', which is being used with an auxiliary, 'has', to form a past tense, used to be known as the past participle. However, this terminology is confusing as this participle can be used to refer to future time also, as in 'After tomorrow, I will have stayed at this hotel five times'.

The '-ed' participle as an adjective

The '-ed' participle can also be used as an adjective: 'the chopped tomatoes', 'the used tickets'. These '-ed' adjectives act as a complement after any form of the verb 'to be':

- the athlete was exhausted;
- the glass was broken (not 'broked', because 'to break' is an irregular verb).

The '-ing' participle acting as part of a verb phrase

If we refer back to the list of auxiliaries above, we find another inflectional ending '-ing'. Forms of the verb that end in '-ing' have traditionally been known as present participles: 'walking', 'sleeping', 'thinking' and so on. However, they function in similar ways to '-ed' participles. They can form a part of a finite form of a verb, so long as they have auxiliaries alongside, to complete a range of tenses: 'I am walking' (present) or 'They were sleeping' (past) or 'We will be thinking' (future).

The '-ing' participle acting as an adjective

'-ing' participles, like '-ed' participles, can also act as adjectives:

- the slithering snake;
- the growling dog;
- the boiling kettle.

The '-ing' participle as a noun

Examples of this usage are:

- Fishing is not allowed in this river.
- My favourite sport is swimming.

It is important to make it clear to children that neither '-ing' participles by themselves nor infinitives (sometimes known as 'base forms') can provide that finite verb form that every sentence must usually have. They can only fulfil this role if they have an auxiliary to help them. In the text 'Class Five were having an outing. Walking along the beach and swimming in the sea', the first sentence is grammatical, because 'having' has an auxiliary with it to help form a past tense. The second sentence is not grammatical because the only forms of verbs that appear in it are '-ing' participles without auxiliaries, 'walking' and 'swimming'. There should be a comma after 'outing' and then 'walking' and 'swimming' can fulfil their roles as adjectives, describing 'Class Five'.

Mood

The indicative mood

So far, nearly all the examples we have given in this section on verbs have been contained in sentences that were making statements.

- The lion is coming.
- I am going tomorrow.

Most verb phrases are in the indicative mood, which is used for making statements. It can also be used for asking questions: 'The lion is coming?' The addition of a question mark tells the reader that the voice rises after coming and the tone is questioning.

The interrogative mood

The questions 'Is the lion coming?' and 'When shall I go?' are different because they have clear question markers inside them. In the first case the word order reveals that a question has been asked: 'Is . . . coming?' In the second, as well as the word order indication, there is also a question word 'When?' These sentences are in the interrogative mood.

The imperative mood

The imperative mood is used when a writer or speaker wants to give suggestions, or orders or instructions (the force behind the imperative will depend very much on the context). If you are doing work on lists with children, or helping them to write recipes or any kind of procedural writing, you will need to draw their attention to the ways in which sentences can be expressed with varying degrees of force in the imperative mood. Frequently the verb comes first and no subject is expressed:

- Break the eggs into the bowl.
- Take a piece of string.
- Go now!

Sometimes teachers try to avoid what might seem like the harshness of the imperative mood by casting their commands or requests in the form of a question instead. 'Shall we put the books away, Robert?' is therefore possibly another way of saying 'Put the books away, Robert, please'. Robert may come unstuck at this point because he has no previous experience of requests being structured in this way. To answer 'No', or even 'No thank you', would not be appropriate.

There is another mood, the subjunctive, that enables the construction of sentences such as 'If I were you, I would not waste time'. It is used very little in modern English.

Active and passive voice

As we have already seen writers or speakers frequently choose to emphasise themselves or their addressee in the way they structure their sentences. They do this by making 'I/we' or 'you' the subject of their sentences. Otherwise, if a more impersonal style of writing is desired, a noun or pronoun in the third person is chosen. In each case we have noticed the pattern of a subject followed by an activity carried out by that subject. Here is an example of a sentence with a third person singular subject, 'birds', a verb in a present tense, 'make', and a noun, 'nests', that is serving as the object of the sentence:

- Birds make nests.

The sentence is written in such a way that readers understand that the subject, the birds, are actively involved in the making. We say that this sentence is in the active voice. One of the features of subject/verb/object sentences, as we have seen already, is that the same meaning can be expressed in another way.

- Nests are made by the birds.

In this version, the 'nests' are now the subject of the sentence, but they do not actually do anything. They have something done to them. This sentence is in the passive voice. The birds are the 'agents'. The events are the same, but they are being described in a different way.

It is possible to have sentences in the passive voice in which the agent is not expressed.

- In spring, nests are made.

Though not particularly significant in this instance, on some occasions it can be very useful to be able to draw a veil over who or what is responsible for something by omitting to mention the agent. Recently, for example, we filled in an important form for our course leader and returned it to her. Some days later she asked for the form again. A number of language choices were open to us. We could have said 'Have you lost the form?', but this would have been unwise. More tactful is 'Has the form been lost?', omitting any mention of an agent. Even this hints at carelessness, and so in the end we opted for 'Has the form disappeared?' As 'to disappear' is an intransitive verb, it manages to convey the idea that somehow the form lost itself (at least we hope so).

It is time now to leave the safe shores of the simple sentence for the more difficult terrain of compound and complex sentences, in which boundaries are hazy and in which thickets of syntax can trap the unwary.

Pause for thought

No, we haven't gone completely mad, nor have we been drinking (it's only 11.30 in the morning). Before starting on the next chapter we are inviting you to have another pause for thought. We would like you to think about your reaction to our change of style in the sentence above. It would be useful if you have read Chapter 4, because in that chapter we raised some issues about structuring different types of text. If you are willing to pause, we would like you to ask yourselves whether you felt irritated by a piece of purple prose in the middle of a section of explanatory text. This might support the theory that language choices are as much about meeting readers' expectations as they are about exploring writers' meanings. You were going along quite nicely following some explanations of points of grammar and syntax, when suddenly you were jolted into something you were not prepared for and which seemed as inappropriate as wearing a dinner jacket on the beach. (It is possible, of course, that you welcomed this break into something more colourful as a pleasing change from what had gone before.)

On the other hand, it may not be the inappropriateness of the style that you object to. It may be that you can't understand a word of what we're talking about. What on earth do we mean by 'thickets of syntax?' You may have no mental image of a thicket, or, if you have, may not see what thickets have to do with syntax. If the chapter is to go on in this vague and imprecise way, you may feel you want none of it. In writing 'thickets of syntax' we are employing a metaphor, and we have more to say about their use (and abuse) in a later chapter.

One final point for you to consider before we try to resume our original explanatory style. One of the syntactic issues we have raised in this chapter is the question of writing in the first, second or third person. We have used first and second person pronouns throughout this book, and we await with interest our publisher's reactions to this. He may decide to chop them all out. Just now, we raised the interpersonal level of the writing quite a bit by telling you that we are writing this at 11.30 in the morning. We tried to force you, in other words, to visualise us for a moment, instead of verbs, nouns or whatever. We would like you to consider the effect of this much more intrusive 'we' at this point in the text. On the whole, adults are meant to know enough about syntactic choices to control the level of 'I/we' and 'you' interference in accordance with the kind of text they are writing. Children take some considerable time to learn this.

Summary

In this chapter we have discussed:

- a definition of grammar;

- written and spoken standard English compared with some regional variations;

- some of the differences between the structure of speech and the structure of writing;

- a range of sentence types;

- the building blocks of sentences:

  - nouns

  - pronouns

  - adjectives

  - articles

  - adverbs

  - verbs.

7

Sentence structure: phrases and clauses

To qualify as a sentence at all, a group of words must contain within it at least one example of a verb in a finite form. We have established in the last chapter that this means one of the forms of a verb that is bounded by tense and person. A sentence with only one finite verb in it is technically known as a simple sentence, or a one-clause sentence. The fact that it is labelled 'simple' does not have anything to do with its length; not all simple sentences are like the sentences we read from the reading scheme. In *Prowlpuss*, by Gina Wilson (1997), we are introduced to the eponymous hero with a terrifying picture of a huge moggy on the first double-page spread. Here is no simple opening sentence to get us off to a gentle start. Gentleness is not what this book is about. We plunge straight in with:

> Prowlpuss is cunning and wily and sly,
> A kingsize cat with one ear and one eye.
> He's not a sit-by-the-fire-and-purr cat,
> A look-at-my-exquisite-fur cat,
> No, he's not!
> He's rough and gruff and very very tough.
> Where ya goin', Prowlpuss?
> AHA

Adjectival phrases

English syntax has been taken by the scruff of the neck in this rhyming story and made to support the author's vivid word picture. The work of describing a noun can be done by a single adjective standing alone,

- 'Prowlpuss is cunning',

but by using a word class that we have not talked about yet, a writer can create a more complex picture by joining several adjectives together into adjectival phrases:

- 'Prowlpuss is cunning and wily and sly'.

A phrase is a group of words working together as a single element in a sentence, in this case to do the work of describing a noun. So we have an adjectival phrase. There is another adjectival phrase in the same sentence, this time describing 'cat':

- '. . . with one ear and one eye'.

Conjunctions

The 'ands' in that adjectival phrase belong to a class of word called conjunctions. The job of all conjunctions is to join sentences or parts of sentences together. 'And' is probably the commonest conjunction of all, though 'or' and 'but' are also frequently used.

These conjunctions are called coordinating conjunctions because all the parts they link together have the same status in the sentence. In our example, 'cunning', 'wily' and 'sly' are all adjectives. It would be possible of course to miss out one or even both of the 'ands':

- Prowlpuss is cunning, wily and sly.

The two 'ands' are another example of an author making syntax serve her meaning; it seems to us that she is piling up the cat's character traits in a very deliberate and emphatic way.

In a spirited approach to conventional grammar that we thoroughly recommend to you, the author has invented her most effective adjectives of all by yoking words together with hyphens to make unique structures, totally unconventional grammatically, but great fun to read:

- 'a sit-by-the-fire-and-purr cat';
- 'a look-at-my-exquisite-fur cat'.

Later on in the text, we are told that Prowlpuss is not

- 'a cuddle-up-for-a-chat cat';
- 'a sit-in-the-window-and-stare cat';
- 'He's an I-WAS-THERE! cat'.

Adverb phrases

Adverb phrases work on the same principle as adjectival ones. Words are combined to do the same work as a single adverb would do. We have mentioned already that adverbs are a word class that can be moved about in a sentence to place the emphasis where the author wants it. Look at this example from later on in Prowlpuss's story:

- 'Back through the alley slinks Prowlpuss at dawn'.

The subject of the sentence is Prowlpuss, but on this occasion the adverb phrase, 'back through the alley', is placed first. It's an adverb phrase of place, because it tells us more about (or modifies) the verb 'slinks'. It tells us where the slinking was done. Putting it first throws quite a lot of emphasis on the phrase and on the word 'slinks'. There is good reason why Prowlpuss is slinking at this point, but we don't want to give too much away.

Noun phrases

Another type of phrase you will frequently encounter is the noun phrase. Noun phrases are groups of words, acting as a unit, that do the same work as single nouns. We have noticed already that the work that nouns do is frequently to be the subject or the object of a sentence. Prowlpuss's owner is called Nellie Smith. Look at the sentence

> And old Nellie Smith in her deep feather bed
> Lifts her head.

The verb in the sentence is 'lifts'. It's interesting that the story is told in the present tense; the past is more usual in a narrative. You might like to speculate on the effect of using a present tense instead. Who does the lifting? Or in other words, who is the subject of the sentence? The group of words 'old Nellie Smith' is filling this slot, a group of words forming a noun phrase. (Are you able to describe what work is being done by the group of words 'in her deep feather bed'?)

Grammar supports meaning making!

We would like to think that children who are offered the kind of spirited reading material they will find in this text (and we have only talked about the grammar; there's much more to enjoy than that) will not grow up afraid of grammar's terrible teeth, but will see it as there to serve speakers and writers in their struggles to express themselves and to have fun with meaning. We cannot emphasise too strongly the importance of approaching grammar through exploring meaning. We can see little point in asking children to 'spot the phrase in line ten' or even to 'make a list of all the adjectival phrases in the story' unless the children can see a reason for doing so. Phrase and clause boundaries are notoriously difficult to define, and we think this is too complex an activity for children in Key Stage 2. But as an adult shares the text with the class, and they enjoy together the vivid picture that is being built up, it would be possible for the adult to pick out some of the phrases, bring them to the children's attention (explaining why they are called phrases) and then discuss with the children how effective they are.

Compound sentences

In all the sentences we have discussed so far there has been only one finite verb. This is why they are all defined as simple sentences. Two simple sentences or one-clause sentences can be joined together using a conjunction. This will form a compound sentence. Each part of a compound sentence could stand alone grammatically. There are various reasons why writers or speakers may want to join them. Speakers, if they are 'in full flow', may not even be conscious that they are doing this. Loosely strung sentences, joined with 'and' or 'but' or 'or', may just pour from them. Writers have more time to think and to revise their sentence shapes. Forming compound sentences may be part of a plan to give a sentence a feeling of balance or to put two sides of a case. Imagine that the following is the opening sentence of a story:

Little Red Riding Hood was a good girl but she really should have paid more attention to her mother's advice.

In the first part of this compound sentence, we have a subject:

- 'Little Red Riding Hood';

and a finite verb:

- 'was'.

In the second part, which is co-equal with the first, we have a subject:

- 'she' (referring back to the previously mentioned Little Red Riding Hood);

and a finite verb:

- 'should have paid'.

Linking the two parts together enables us to consider two facets of her character. Little Red Riding Hood is to be the heroine of the story, so we want to engage the readers' sympathies for her; on the other hand, she did have a weakness, and this is what will lead to the complication in her story.

From a non-fiction text, *Time and Space* by Mary and John Gribbin (1994), we have another example of the way a compound sentence allows writers to hold two ideas in relation to each other. The writers have been making the point that we seem to move through – or with – time, but always in the same direction:

We cannot go back for a second to look at the past, nor can we jump forward for a preview of the future.

'Nor' is the conjunction here. It is a rather literary conjunction, very seldom used in spoken English. Notice how it requires an inversion of the finite verb after it.

Children tend to use the conjunction 'and' very indiscriminately in their writing, and sometimes it's difficult to explain to them how to edit some of them out. Children in Key Stage 2 should be encouraged to justify the use of the word in their texts. If they can't find a reason for a particular 'and' it would be worth seeing whether the text sounds better without it.

Complex sentences

In order to begin to understand complex sentences we need to return to the three word classes we have met twice before already:

- adjectives;
- adverbs;
- nouns.

You should by now be fairly clear about the work that each of these word classes does in sentences. You will also remember that this work can be done

- by single adjectives, adverbs or nouns: 'She has written a simple story' (adjective), 'They crept slowly towards the hut' (adverb), 'Jack fell down' (noun);
- by groups of words acting together to form a phrase. 'She has written a simple story with a brilliant ending' (adjectival phrase), 'They crept towards the hut on their hands and knees' (adverbial phrase), 'That good-for-nothing Jack fell down' (noun phrase).

Subordinate clauses

It is also possible to insert into sentences groups of words that do the work of adverbs, adjectives and nouns, and which have their own subject and their own finite verb. Because they have a finite verb, they are not phrases, but clauses.

In complex sentences, there is only one clause that could, in theory, make sense by itself. It is known as the main clause. The other clauses are dependent upon, or relate to, the main clause in some way or other. They are known as subordinate clauses.

- A complex sentence is technically a sentence with a main clause and at least one subordinate clause.

It need not be very long or 'complex' in the non-technical sense, just as a so-called 'simple' sentence can actually be quite long and involved. However, some writers are masters (or mistresses) of the complex sentence, and can weave clauses together so beautifully that half the pleasure of reading their work is in appreciating their beautiful cadences. Jane Austen is an obvious example. Here is the opening sentence from *Persuasion*:

> Sir Walter Elliot, of Kellynch-hall in Somersetshire, was a man who, for his own amusement, never took up any book but the Baronetage; there he found occupation for an idle hour, and consolation in a distressed one; there his faculties were roused into admiration and respect, by contemplating the limited remnant of the earliest patents; there any unwelcome sensations, arising from domestic affairs, changed naturally into pity and contempt, as he turned over the almost endless creations of

the last century – and there, if every other leaf were powerless, he could read his own history with an interest which never failed.

This kind of complex sentence would sound very odd in a spoken text, and yet it is what gives the writing its unique flavour.

Types of subordinate clause

Relative clauses

Consider the sentence 'She has written a simple story which will delight all young readers'. In this expanded version of what started off as a simple sentence, we now have two pieces of information about the story:

- it is simple;
- it will delight all young readers.

There are two clauses because there are two finite verbs, 'has written' and 'will delight'. In this example, 'which' relates all the words that come after it to the one word 'story'. In old-fashioned clause analysis, this group of words would have been described as an adjectival phrase. Nowadays, it would be labelled a 'relative clause'. This label is more appropriate because, introduced as they are by relative pronouns, it is possible for relative clauses to do work other than describing nouns. For example, in the sentence 'He is working hard, which is a miracle', 'which' relates everything after it to everything that has gone before.

Relative clauses can also be introduced by the relative pronouns 'who' and 'that':

- Susan, who is my mother's cousin, has gone to live in Australia.
- This is the book that I told you about.

In both of these examples, the relative clauses are giving more information about nouns – 'Susan' and 'book'. In these particular cases they are therefore acting adjectivally.

Adverbial clauses

Subordinate adverbial clauses do similar work to adverbs and adverbial phrases. The sentence 'They crept towards the hut' makes perfect sense as it stands. It could be a one-clause sentence. However, the person writing this text would probably feel under pressure to explain why this unusual activity was taking place: 'They crept towards the hut because they were afraid of being seen'. The one-clause sentence has now become the main clause of a complex sentence, and a subordinate clause has been added.

This second clause, because it does the work of explaining why the 'creeping' was going on, is an adverbial clause of reason. Like its cousin, the single adverb, it can move about in the sentence, depending on where the writer wants to put the emphasis. 'Because they were afraid of being seen, they crept towards the hut' is just as acceptable grammatically, though many inexperienced readers find it difficult to cope with sentences in which too many words come before the main subject. To be able to cope with and enjoy the effect of sentences such as the latter version is another test of a child's developing literary prowess.

Noun clauses

There is one other form of subordination that you need to be aware of, in which the subordinate clause fulfils a role similar to that performed by nouns or pronouns:

- I said those words.
- I said that you may go to the party. (object)
- It is not important.
- What you did is not important. (subject)
- Take it to her.
- Take it to whoever is waiting for it.

Clauses in context

We would advocate the same approach to work on clauses as we have suggested for phrases. 'Spotting the clauses' is meaningless unless there is some discussion linked to their use. In the following extract from *The Lion, the Witch and the Wardrobe*, C.S. Lewis (1980: 11) is establishing the first setting for his fantasy story, the house from which the children will pass through into Narnia.

> It was the sort of house that you never seem to come to the end of, and it was full of unexpected places. The first few doors they tried led only into spare bedrooms, as everyone had expected that they would; but soon they came to a very long room full of pictures and there they found a suit of armour; and after that was a room all hung with green, with a harp in one corner; and then came three steps down and five steps up, and then a kind of little upstairs hall and a door that led out on to a balcony, and then a whole series of rooms that led into each other and were lined with books – most of them very old books and some bigger than a Bible in a church. And shortly after that they looked into a room that was quite empty except for one big wardrobe; the sort that has a looking-glass in the door. There was nothing else in the room at all except a dead blue-bottle on the window sill.
> 'Nothing there!' said Peter, and they all trooped out again – all except Lucy.

There's quite an array of 'ands' here, but all thoroughly justified. No one would want to list all the phrases and clauses, but what we can do is to draw the passage to children's attention, and show them how well the sentence structure matches the house the writer is describing. For example, the second sentence, which is very long indeed, matches with its twists and turns the twisting passages and the rooms leading off one another that characterise the building. Punctuation is vital to prevent the reader from getting lost in the sentence: it contains three semicolons, four commas and a dash!

When we come to the next sentence (the one beginning with 'and'!) we have quite a different structure, in which a few phrases are allowed to stand out sharply:

- 'quite empty';
- 'one big wardrobe'.

The next sentence is even more stark in its simplicity:

- 'There was nothing else in the room at all' (except for the dead blue-bottle, which is a touch of genius; it doesn't detract from the stark simplicity, but adds to it).

The word 'nothing' in that sentence is picked up again, and reinforced, when it is put into the mouth of Peter – and so we as readers are on a knife-edge: will the magic be discovered or not?

To talk about the writer's skill in weaving different sentence structures together is very different from picking out the clauses with a highlighter pen, a difficult and soul-destroying task. The children can be introduced to the jargon:

- phrase;
- clause;
- simple sentence;
- compound sentence;
- complex sentence.

But the most important aspect of the discussion is to appreciate what a skilful writer can do with these structures. It may also be that some children will be encouraged to have a go at a more deliberate use of subordinate clauses as a result of such explicit discussion, or may be helped to see how they can increase the flow of their sentences by incorporating some of the information they want to convey in subordinate clauses.

Cohesion and connection

Grammar, as we have been at pains to explain in this chapter and the last, is the speaker's or writer's tool enabling meaning to be structured and expressed in a variety of subtle ways. Though some indulgence is shown to speakers if speed and spontaneity render them a little bit incoherent, writers and indeed speakers who have time to rehearse will go to some trouble to make their texts 'cohesive' or, in other words, to ensure that each bit of their meaning is somehow bound into the whole so that readers or listeners can follow their drift, and can see the connections between one sentence or one part of the text and another. We can illustrate this by asking you to look back at the extract from *The Lion, the Witch and the Wardrobe*.

Conjunctions

Conjunctions come immediately to mind when we think of joining parts of a text together, and indeed they are important, though they are by no means the only way of forming cohesive links. In the first sentence of the extract, for example, C.S. Lewis provides two pieces of information about the house, both of equal importance, so he links them together with 'and':

- 'It was the sort of house that you never seem to come to the end of, and it was full of unexpected places.'

Sometimes, the writer wants to provide contrastive information and so 'but' is a more useful conjunction:

- 'The first few doors they tried led only into spare bedrooms, as everyone had expected that they would; but soon they came to a very long room full of pictures.'

Adverbs as cohesive ties

Adverbs provide strong links in a text, allowing a variety of connections between items. Here they are largely temporal, though there is one spatial connection:

- 'soon they came to a very long room . . .' (temporal link);
- 'after that there was a room . . .' (ditto);
- 'and then came . . .' (ditto);
- 'and then a kind of . . .' (ditto);
- 'and then a whole series . . .' (ditto);
- 'shortly after that . . .' (ditto);
- 'there they found a suit of armour . . .' (spatial link).

Pronouns

Pronouns allow writers to make referential connections back to people or things mentioned earlier in the text:

- 'it [the house] was full of unexpected places. The first few doors they [the children] tried led only into spare bedrooms.'

Ellipsis

Sometimes words, or even longer parts of sentences, can be omitted because the writer assumes that his or her readers will carry some meaning forward:

- 'one big wardrobe; the sort ['of wardrobe' omitted] that has a looking-glass in the door.'

- 'The first few doors . . . led only into spare bedrooms, as everyone had expected that they would ['lead' omitted].'

Lexical cohesion

Words can be repeated, exemplifying one type of what is known as lexical cohesion:

- 'rooms that led into each other and were lined with books – most of them very old books and some ['books' omitted] bigger than a Bible in a church.'

Another type of lexical cohesion is represented by the 'books . . . Bible' link. Writers can achieve cohesiveness in their texts by using words that collocate, or 'keep company with each other' (for more on collocation, see pp. 87–8).

Readers must work hard to make cohesive links

Writers come to expect a fair amount of skill and expertise from readers with regard to such things as filling the gaps left by elided meanings, looking back to find a referent previously mentioned, or carrying a word or phrase forward in the mind until it is referred to a little while later in the text. The nature of the cohesive ties will very much depend on the type of text. In a recipe, for example, some of the cohesion might be provided by numbering each stage in the process. Sometimes writers delight in omitting cohesive ties, leaving the reader with a lot of detective work to do. This wealth of connectives and cohesive ties can take some time for children to become familiar with in reading, let alone to make use of in their own texts.

It would be impossible in two chapters to explore all the highways and byways of English grammar. There are those who delight in arguing over a particular usage or analysing an obscure example. This is to make grammar an end in itself and for some it is a life's work. In primary schools we think the task is not to seek out the difficult or the obscure example, but to make clear the basic principles on which text is constructed, in the hope that this will serve the more important ends of meaning making and sharing.

Summary

In this chapter we have discussed:

- phrases (adjectival/adverbial/noun);

- compound sentences;

- complex sentences and types of subordinate clause (relative/adverbial/noun/ methods of achieving cohesion in a text).

Activity 3: Audit your sentence-level knowledge

1. What kind of sentence is each of the following?

    (a) What would it have been like to have lived when dinosaurs ruled the earth?
    (b) Our class enjoyed our trip to Chester Zoo and we would like to go again.
    (c) Make a nose using papier-mâché.
    (d) Let them enjoy a long and prosperous life!

2. Identify each of the sentences in (1) as simple, compound or complex.

3. *Punctuation*. Very few sentences consist of combinations of single words. An example of one that does would be 'I live here'. It's more usual to find 'chunking' of words with some, though by no means all, of the chunks marked by some form of punctuation. An example would be 'I/have lived/in London/ for many years'. We've rewritten one of the dinosaur sentences, leaving out the punctuation:

    > Imagine the sight and smell of a herd of 40-tonne Brachiosaurus in a conifer forest pine needles showering down from their munching mouths 14 metres above you.

    (a) Indicate by a line where you think the chunks might begin and end.
    (b) Punctuate the passage.
    (c) Here is another reconstruction from the same text. What do you think about the changes we have made to the punctuation, replacing the full stop after 'view' with a comma?

    > Recent discoveries have shattered this view, we now know that dinosaurs were a great success.

4. Which voice (active or passive) is being used in the italicised part of the sentence: 'When the cocoa beans are dry, *they are packed into sacks*'.

5. From the sentences in (1) identify:

    (a) an imperative verb;
    (b) a verb in the infinitive.

6. *Word classes* (you may be used to calling these 'parts of speech'). When you are deciding which class of words a particular example belongs to, it's very important to look at the word in the context of the other words around it. Look again at this sentence: 'No book can really show you'.

    (a) What class of words does 'book' belong to here?
    (b) Can you put the word 'book' into two other sentences, in each of which it belongs to a different class of words?

7. *Standard and non-standard English*. Would you say that you spoke using standard English? Sometimes? Always? Do you use standard English when you are writing?

   (a)   Are you clear about what the term refers to?
   (b)   Explain the difference between accent and dialect.
   (c)   In the following extract, what language features suggest that the novel is written in a regional dialect?

   > Now then, I was twelve, rising thirteen, when our Daniel got killed. Aye . . . it was a long time ago. I'm talking about a time of day eighty-three years back. Eighty-three years. It's a time of day that's past your imagining.

See pages 164–6 for a commentary on these activities.

8

Words, words, words

Ask someone what they think of as 'language development' and vocabulary is likely to be one of the first things they mention. When we ask new students – or children – why we learn to read, frequently the first reason either group give is 'to learn new words' (from the children) or 'to increase our vocabulary' (might be the way the students put it). When we look at the aims listed in the language policies of some schools, we often see the same priority. Here is a typical policy:

> As language is so important when working with young children our aims are to:
>
> - help them develop a good vocabulary;
> - encourage them to articulate and speak clearly;
> - help them to acquire the ability to retell and explain what they are doing;
> - help them to be able to repeat rhymes and stories;
> - encourage them to use their imaginations to tell their own stories;
> - help them learn how to hold a conversation with friends and adults – listen as well as talk;
> - encourage them to explain how they feel;
> - encourage them to express their own opinions.

These are all worthwhile language aims, but we would like to turn them round a bit and to combine the elements in different ways. The sixth point holds the key to it all.

Starting from an interesting context

As young children build up confidence in conversing, first with family and friends and then with a wider circle of adults, explaining how they feel, expressing their own opinions, listening to others as well as talking, they will find more and more things to talk about. They may talk about where they have been, about something they have been told, or about what they have seen on television. They may try out some of the words they have heard others use, they will receive feedback and extension of their ideas from supportive adults and hence, gradually, they will develop a wider vocabulary – words that they can use again and again. This vocabulary will largely be of the 'everyday' sort: the nouns, verbs, adjectives and so on that we use to gossip, to mull over events, to describe our plans, to make requests and so on.

Finding the 'right' words

Building up their everyday vocabulary is not without its difficulties and dangers for some children. Precisely because a word seems so ordinary, so rooted in everyday experience for an adult, he or she may be proportionately more outraged by a child who uses a different word. We have never forgotten a discussion we had with a teacher from a South Yorkshire school who was adamant that no child in her class was going to write under her picture, 'This is me playing with my mates', though this is an everyday word for 'friends' in that area. Children are often criticised for using vocabulary that seems to a teacher limited or regional or impolite – as in the requests for going to the toilet mentioned on page 32. We remember another angry teacher declaring, 'I will not have them coming in in the morning and saying "Wotcher, miss!"'

This is not to deny a teacher the right to negotiate in his or her classroom how greetings, requests for the toilet, and so on will be expressed. But it is a plea for careful and sympathetic handling of these issues. The vocabulary of school can require some getting used to, as can the need to be more explicit and to speak more clearly and distinctly than is often necessary at home. However, the urge to join in these everyday classroom conversations will be a powerful incentive to get the pitch and volume to the acceptable standard, to remember to look someone in the eye, and to smile at the right moment. All these add up to a complex set of expectations and take some time to get right. Many an adult has never done so.

Shared worlds, shared words

The words we use to talk or write to people we know well are deeply rooted in shared experience. One word in such a context can carry as much meaning as a dozen words to someone we scarcely know. Children have been part of these shared implicit meanings since they were born, but it will take some time before they are conscious of how the degree of explicitness when dealing with a topic must be adjusted depending on the context and the audience.

The words of songs and rhymes

So far, we have been talking about spoken vocabulary of an unrehearsed kind – used in those contexts in which speech is very different from writing. In addition to these words, some children will come to school knowing words they have learned in rhymes and counting games. Some will already have a repertoire of favourite songs and stories. Teachers need to build on these experiences so that all the children meet words of another sort from the everyday ones:

- 'Ring a ring o' roses, a pocket full of posies';
- 'Hickory, dickory, dock';

- 'Little Miss Muffett sat on her tuffet'.

They may not be sure what some of these words mean. What exactly happened to Jack when he fell down and 'broke his crown'? What, for that matter, was the 'pail' of water he went up the hill to fetch? But in these cases, not knowing the exact meaning of the words does not spoil the pleasure of joining in the songs and rhymes; the words will largely be used in the specific context of singing or reciting. It may never come to light that the meanings are a bit of a mystery.

Words encountered in stories

Favourite stories are a different case again. Here we do all want to share in the meanings that are being explored, but the words that are used are often not the same as the ones for everyday use, or if they are they are combined in ways different from those heard at the breakfast table or the bus stop:

> Once upon a time, there was a dark, dark moor. On the moor was a dark, dark wood. In the wood, there was a dark, dark house. At the front of the house, there was a dark, dark door.
>
> (Brown 1992)

A tired parent, wanting to get out of reading a bedtime story, might try to get away with a retelling: 'We've had this one before: you remember there was a box, in a corner of a cupboard, behind a curtain, along a passage . . .' It just won't do. What we have here is not a boring repetitious use of the word 'dark'; here we have the opportunity to scare ourselves witless, even though we've heard the story many times before and we know there's only a mouse at the end. The repetition of the word, together with the wonderful illustrations, work on us like a spell.

Words can't come out of nothing

To return to the views with which we opened this chapter, it is unwise to see the growth of vocabulary as a first priority in language development. What we are dealing with here is another example of the necessity for a 'top-down' perspective on the growth of language knowledge. Vocabulary – whether of the everyday, bread and butter variety, or of the more literary kinds – grows slowly out of experience – experience of talking and listening and reading, and then experimenting with writing. If the experience has been a good one, or a challenging one, making new demands on us, we are more likely to remember some of the new words that helped us to come to terms with it. But there is little or no chance of remembering any words if the experience was contrived. There is even less likelihood if no experience at all was provided, and the word work was merely part of a set of decontextualised language exercises.

What do we mean by a contrived experience? The teacher who responds to a spring morning by asking the children for all the words they can think of to describe it, writes the words on the board and then encourages the class to incorporate as many of these words as possible into a poem is unlikely to add very much to any pupil's permanent vocabulary.

Drama and role play

To emphasise the quality of experience does not necessarily mean that all the experience must be first-hand. It is very difficult, for example, to give children first-hand experience of finding the appropriate vocabulary to negotiate with powerful adults. Role play is one way of doing it. Through improvised drama after a shared story, children can be required, for example, to conjure up the words to persuade the cowardly king to lead his army into battle. Film and television are likely to offer today's children some of their most powerful experiences – as, of course, are reading and being read to. In choosing to share any of these with children, the criterion uppermost in our minds should not be the growth in vocabulary that may result, but the quality of the experience that the text, whether media text or written, provides. We want to know more about space, or dinosaurs, or King Henry VIII. We want to know how to look after guinea pigs. We want to give ourselves a thrill or a fright or a good laugh. Quality texts can offer all of these and will at the same time provide new words for our consideration.

The danger of working from extracts

There is sometimes a danger of plundering a text for suitable extracts in order to explore aspects of grammar or vocabulary, perhaps to discuss how a character has been delineated or a setting described. When this happens, we are back to something akin to a decontextualised exercise. Though it's not part of our brief to discuss classroom approaches in this book, we would like to make it clear that we can see little merit in offering children isolated extracts from a text. Every child needs to start from the experience of the film or the book as a whole. If a book is to be the basis of some shared work, it may be read aloud by the teacher and may be edited to fit into a certain number of shared reading sessions. Some children may be encouraged to read it independently and to read other texts for comparison and contrast. We can help children to become more explicitly aware of how writers achieve their effects through skilful use of text structure, sentence shapes and choice of words. But in 'numbering the streaks on the tulip' we must be very careful indeed that we don't lose sight of the whole flower.

Having made our position clear, we hope, we can now go on to show how an interest in words, and an enthusiasm for trying them out in one's own work, might grow from shared reading of quality texts.

Word-level work based on *The Wind in the Willows*

We mentioned the possibility of writing about spring earlier in this chapter. There is an opportunity to look closely at how an established children's author, Kenneth Grahame, has tackled this in *The Wind in the Willows* (1983). In Chapter 1, Mole has emerged from a heavy bout of spring cleaning and is going for a walk:

It all seemed too good to be true. Hither and thither through the meadows he rambled busily, along the hedgerows, across the copses, finding everywhere birds building, flowers budding, leaves thrusting – everything happy and progressive and occupied . . . He thought his happiness was complete when, as he meandered aimlessly along, suddenly he stood by the edge of a full-fed river. Never in his life had he seen a river before – this sleek, sinuous, full-bodied animal, chasing and chuckling, gripping things with a gurgle and leaving them with a laugh, to fling itself on fresh playmates that shook themselves free and were caught and held again. All was a-shake and a-shiver – glints and gleams and sparkles, rustle and swirl, chatter and bubble.

Grahame (1983: 8)

Synonyms, connotation and denotation

One place to start thinking about this text at the word level might be with the words Kenneth Grahame has used instead of 'going for a walk'. We are first of all told that Mole

- 'rambled busily'.

Later on he

- 'meandered aimlessly'.

'Ramble' and 'meander' are synonyms of 'walk'. A synonym is defined as a word that means the same as another. In fact, no two words ever do mean exactly the same thing to a native speaker. Their dictionary or 'lexical' meaning may be the same. That is, they may label or 'denote' the same activity, quality or object. In this case, the words denote putting one foot in front of another and moving along. The denotation of words is probably their least interesting aspect, however. As we read this passage, Mole first rambling and then meandering will conjure up for each reader different ways of 'putting one foot in front of another and moving along'. That is to say, the words will have a variety of connotations, or personal associations, for each of us. This will depend to some extent on our age, interests, attitudes to walking and so on. Of course, among readers who share a social and cultural background, there are likely to be a lot of shared connotations.

Kenneth Grahame has elaborated on the two synonyms, 'rambled' and 'meandered', by adding adverbs after them. Mole 'rambled busily' and he 'meandered aimlessly'. This to some extent controls the readers' reactions more tightly – keeps their imaginations within bounds. As it happens, the connotations we bring to the words are just those the adverbs seem to reinforce. Ramblers are energetic people in shorts and hiking boots, whereas those who meander are much less purposive. We imagine them in sandals with floppy hats on their heads. (Though not Mole, we hasten to add.)

Words carry emotional overtones

Frequently words are carefully chosen so that their connotations might conjure up an emotional response in the mind of the reader or listener, might persuade them to look at an issue from the writer's or the speaker's angle. Before any words are written, or put into a prepared talk, a considerable amount of mental work takes place. The speaker or writer hopes to tap into shared experiences with the reader or listener, in terms of not just everyday life, but shared history, shared reading, films, TV programmes and so on. They can never be sure, of course, exactly what the effect of their words will be.

Figurative language

Figurative language is very prevalent in everyday life, although it's possibly something you have associated more with literature, especially poetry. We hear a lot on the news at the moment about 'the climate of fear' that prevails in some parts of the world, and terrorist acts are referred to by some commentators as 'stoking the fires of hatred'. One of the most interesting aspects of the passage from *The Wind in the Willows* is the choice of words used to describe the river. It is seen by Mole as an animal, sleek, sinuous and full-bodied. To describe something as if it were something else, calling the supermarket's suppliers the slaves, or a river an animal, is to use a metaphor. If the writer had used a comparative word – if he had said that the river looked 'like' an animal, he would have been using a simile. These are types of what is known as figurative language. The connotations of the words used in the metaphors are interesting to consider. What kinds of associations are conjured up in your mind by the words 'sleek' and 'sinuous'?

Collocation, onomatopoeia, alliteration

Once we have been introduced to the idea of the river as an animal, we can look for other words that follow up the metaphor, that keep company with the 'animal' idea. Words that frequently go together are said to 'collocate'. Is the river a wild animal? A playful animal? A pet? All these ideas might collocate with 'animal' in the minds of most of us. Well, it seems too lively for a pet, but more 'boisterous' than 'wild'. It 'flings itself on fresh playmates', though they don't seem too concerned, shaking themselves free, but then being caught and held again. There is 'laughter', and synonyms for laughter, 'chuckling' and 'gurgling'. In building up the picture of the river, Kenneth Grahame uses a lot of onomatopoeic words. This term refers to words that actually suggest the sounds they represent: chuckling; gripping things with a gurgle; rustle and swirl; a-shake and a-shiver; chatter and bubble. Some of these words are alliterative. 'Alliteration' is a term you are likely to have come across, meaning the repetition of a sound, usually the initial one, for a particular purpose or effect.

The sounds conjured up by the onomatopoeia and the alliteration are busy, energetic sounds, such as 'rustle' and 'swirl', rather than, say, 'roar' or 'growl', so they add something to the kind of animal picture we were building earlier. We spoke in the last chapter of various kinds of grammatical cohesion, which help to give a unified feel to a text. We have here a good example of lexical cohesion, which has the same effect.

The words we have picked out for comment, because they collocate happily with each other, make the piece hang together. We can build a picture of the river in our minds that makes sense to us.

Morphology

Another way of looking at this text at the word level would be to consider the structures of some of the words. The study of word structure is called morphology. A word's structure can be changed by adding letters to the beginning of the word (a prefix) or to the end (a suffix). Adding suffixes frequently changes the grammatical work a word does, and we have looked at some of these endings in the grammar chapter. If you have read that chapter, you might like to take a minute to consider whether there are any significant word endings you recognise in this passage before reading on.

One suffix you might have recognised was '-ing'. Kenneth Grahame mentions birds 'building', flowers 'budding' and leaves 'thrusting', and there are several more examples later on: 'chasing' and 'chuckling'; 'gripping' and 'leaving'. As we have several times pleaded in this book, do avoid the trap of playing games of 'spot the (in this case) -ing participle' with children. This is of no use at all unless you go on to discuss the effect the words have on the reader. And of course, although we can all be reasonably sure, after a while, of what an -ing participle is, the effect on the reader is much more open to interpretation. This is one of the most important lessons that children can learn as they become more advanced readers, and you should go out of your way to encourage them to decide for themselves, after due consideration of the evidence, why the writer has made this grammatical choice. We'll refrain therefore from describing what the effect is on us, lest it should be taken by some readers as the definitive answer!

Morphemes

We have looked at two examples of suffixes in this passage, that is, letters or groups of letters that can be added to the ends of words to change their grammatical function:

- '-ing' has been added to words like 'build' and 'bud' and 'thrust';
- 's' has been added to words like 'glint' and 'gleam' and 'sparkle'.

This means that all these words now consist of two morphemes. David Crystal (1987: 90) refers to morphemes as 'the smallest building blocks in the grammar of a language'. There are two kinds.

Free morphemes

The six words quoted above – 'build', 'bud' and so on – can stand alone or can be used as part of many other words: 'builder' or 'disbud' or 'gleamed', for example. In their original root form they are called free morphemes.

Bound morphemes

The other parts of the words, '-ing' and 's' and 'er' and 'dis' and 'ed', could not stand alone. They are called bound morphemes because they can only be found attached to free morphemes. Bound morphemes can be used to change the grammatical status of a word: 'er' changes 'build' from a verb to a noun, for example; 'ed' changes 'gleam' into a past tense. Bound morphemes can also be used to change the meaning of a word: 'dis' prefixed to 'bud' turns the word into something that means the opposite of the original.

Building our own word hoards

Before leaving the passage we would like to return briefly to the question of increasing the reader's own vocabulary as a result of the experience of reading this text. A lot of the words in it are no longer current, even in fiction: words such as 'hither' and 'thither' or 'playmates' or 'a-shake' and 'a-shiver'. These are a bit like museum pieces: interesting to look at, but not for current use. Some words, however, may be picked out by readers for further use. 'Meandered' is one that appeals to us, and that we might be tempted to try out when the opportunity arose. Whether it would stay active in our writing or speaking for long is another matter.

Building up one's personal word collection is rather like going for walks on a pebbly beach after the tide has gone out. There are lots of attractive stones lying around and we might be tempted to rush around picking them up. Yet very few will ever gain a permanent place on the shelf. Some will be dropped before leaving the beach, and even some of those that are taken home will lurk in the garage or a dark place in the garden, never really to be looked at again. Yet we will have enjoyed them all, however fleetingly; the colour, the texture, the feel of them. Children should be allowed to meet and enjoy words in a variety of contexts. Some they need not decode independently, or remember how to spell, for a long time after meeting them, if ever.

The attraction of unusual words

As we have implied in our comments about nursery rhymes, words can fascinate us and mesmerise us, even though we find them difficult to understand. Marcus, a teenage character in the novel *Still Life* by A.S. Byatt (1985), starts to recover from the chronic depression he has been suffering through the unlikely remedy of A-level botany. The author states that, after months of not being able to involve himself in anything, he 'wrote quietly about the monoecious and dioecious households of trees and the extravagant mimetic capacities of the bee orchid' (p. 363). She goes on to ask: 'From where does the intense satisfaction come, that is to be taken in that kind of writing?' (p. 363). Or more simply, in listing and drawing as Marcus did:

Alopecurus – Fox-tail grass
Phalaris – Canary grass
Phleum – Cat's-tail grass . . .

(Byatt 1985: 363)

The list goes on. What has a fascination for botanical terms got to do with primary children? An interest in jargon, in technical terms, is not something that comes only in the secondary phase of schooling. The words in books like Stephen Biesty's, for example, will probably fascinate some Key Stage 2 readers far more powerfully than those in a story or poem ever will. Here, for example, is an extract from *Stephen Biesty's Incredible Everything* (2000: 18) describing part of a Boeing 777:

> The 777 is a 'fly-by-wire' aircraft. Controls in the cockpit are not linked directly to the 'flight feathers' (control surfaces such as the ailerons, rudder and elevators). Instead, the pilot's sidestick sends signals to a computer system, which adjusts the aircraft's direction and altitude.

Even the very young reader can find technical terms fascinating. In stage one of Ginn's 'All Aboard' reading scheme, beginner readers are introduced to a non-fiction book, *Honeybee*. On pages 6 and 7, we find a large drawing of the bee's three body parts, labelled 'head', 'thorax' and 'abdomen'. 'Pupae' and 'antennae' are also labelled on other pages, along with 'tongue', 'legs', 'wings' and 'eyes'. But although all these words may be savoured at the time of reading, they will not necessarily stay in the reader's mind for long.

Controlled vocabulary

This attitude to introducing specialised vocabulary in the earliest stages of reading represents a radical departure from that frequently mocked approach to beginning reading which took the same twelve words and used them over and over again: 'Here is Peter and here is Jane. Jane is here and Peter is here . . .' and so on ad nauseam. This strange kind of text arose from too rigid an adherence to the notion of 'controlled vocabulary'. In the 'Look and Say' approach to reading, children were not required to break words down into their constituent sounds, but to remember them as wholes. New words were only introduced very gradually as the scheme progressed; they had a high rate of repetition and were carried over to following books in the series.

Key words

The Ladybird reading scheme that featured Peter and Jane was based on careful research into 'key words', the name given to a group of the most used words in the language (Murray 1969). The research established that relatively few English words make up a very high proportion of those in everyday use. It was calculated that 20,000 words form the vocabulary of an average adult and, of these, twelve key words make up a quarter of all the words we read and write. One hundred key words make up half of those in common use. It seemed very sensible, then, to build a set of early reading books on the basis of the gradual introduction of a few more key words each time, until children felt confident enough to read them.

One unfortunate aspect of this approach is that the most frequently used words are, not surprisingly, 'bread and butter' words of no great colour or excitement. The first twelve are 'a', 'and', 'he', 'I', 'in', 'is', 'it', 'of', 'that', 'the', 'to' and 'was'. They have little or no colourful content, though they all play a vital role in the construction of sentences. They are an interesting set in a number of ways, not least because, although 'he' is in the list, 'she' isn't!

Nowadays, although key words are still a feature of modern reading schemes, writers of reading scheme material are urged to introduce them more naturally, alongside more exciting content words. The key words do need to be learned as quickly as possible, because they occur so frequently, but writers are free to introduce children to a wide variety of other words at the same time. Sometimes we find that students are still confused about the difference between these two categories of words, and avoid using a text with young children because it has some difficult words in it that beginner readers might not understand. These words, to return to the earlier metaphor, are frequently the more colourful 'pebbles' that may be picked up very briefly and quickly discarded, but are likely to provide an interesting experience. Provided the text is being shared with a sensitive adult who knows what kinds of support to provide, they will not be off-putting at all.

Children need to meet exciting words!

A point that we made in the grammar chapter holds true for words too. Children need to encounter writers who know how to be bold or innovative with words. In *Dinosaur Roar* (2005), a picture book by Paul and Henrietta Stickland, the verbs are 'roar', 'squeak', 'gobble', 'nibble', 'munch' and 'scrunch'. We would call this a bold bunch. The adjectives in the book are bold, too, and what is also helpful for young readers is that they help readers to see the dinosaurs in pairs of opposites, a concept that young children often find difficult to grasp. 'Dinosaur short', for example, can be compared with 'dinosaur very, very long', and 'dinosaur fat' with 'dinosaur tiny'.

Having fun with words

There are many texts in which the chief aim is to have fun with words. A good example of this kind of text is *Don't Put Your Finger in the Jelly, Nelly* by Nick Sharratt (2005). Photographs of various messy foods are very cleverly combined into illustrations of plates, bowls, paper bags, and so on, and by means of a series of judiciously placed holes it is possible to create the illusion of poking one's finger into such things as a large jelly, a lemon meringue pie, a piece of cheese and a bowl of pasta.

The fun comes when you turn over the page and find your finger is caught in the trunk of a 'jellyphant', or has been grabbed by a 'meringue-utan', or has woken up the 'spag-yeti'.

Invented words

A well-known example of invented words is Lewis Carroll's *Jabberwocky*:

Twas brillig and the slithy toves
Did gyre and gimble in the wabe;
All mimsy were the borogroves,
And the mome raths outgrabe.

(Gardner 1972: 730)

Discussing this text provides a wonderful opportunity to compare the connotations that the words have for each reader. We can't look the words up in a dictionary and so we are thrown back on associations, particularly associations with the sounds the words make – the onomatopoeic element of words that we referred to earlier. Lewis Carroll apparently formed 'brillig' by combining the two words 'boiling' and 'grilling' and had in mind a particular time of day when the evening meal was being cooked. To us, however, the words always suggest a description of the weather: a picture of bright sunshine and stifling heat, with the slithy toves trying to keep cool by gyring and gimbling. (How many prefixes and suffixes can you attach to 'gyre' and 'gimble'? 'Disgyre'? Or 'ungimble'? What would they mean?)

Phonology

Finally in this chapter we want to say something about the smallest units of all of the English language – the sounds. Phonology is the name given to the study of the sound system of a language. A phonic strategy, when helping children to decode a word in a text, involves breaking a word down into its constituent sounds and then blending them together to make the whole word. Phonological awareness, the awareness of speech as a sequence of separable sounds rather than a stream of meaning, takes a long time to develop in some children. Pre-readers especially have largely experienced language as a continuous stream of sounds in which the word boundaries, let alone the sound boundaries, are very difficult to detect. But it is not only they who struggle. Take for instance the child (he was in Key Stage 2) who wrote about the 'warmer morial'. He had never seen the words written down and had no clear idea of what they represented. One of us taught in London, where children used to write that they had been cycling up 'Blackifill' (Blackheath Hill) at the weekend. The difficulty is compounded here by the fact that the children spoke with a south London accent, which rendered /th/ as /ff/. (// around letters of the alphabet or phonic symbols means that a sound is being referred to.) Try to put yourself in the children's place by listening to a conversation between native speakers in a language you don't speak fluently. Can you detect the word boundaries?

Phonemes

When we come to the boundaries between the sounds, the difficulties are even greater. Pause for a moment and consider how many sounds you can hear in 'physical', 'frightened' or 'transport'. (You can check in the note at the end of the chapter if you are not sure.) The human voice is capable of producing a very large range of sounds, especially if we take into account sounds produced with a rising note or with a falling note. In some languages, this difference in intonation is sufficient to signal a difference in meaning. Fortunately for us, this is not the case in English. In English spoken with a received pronunciation accent (see p. 53) there are forty-four sounds that can cause a change of meaning. By this we mean that when native speakers hear 'pin' and 'bin' clearly articulated, or 'cat' and 'cap', they will agree that two distinct objects have been referred to. These forty-four basic units of sound are called phonemes. There are twenty vowel phonemes and twenty-four consonant phonemes. It's not easy to write sounds down without having recourse to a phonetic alphabet, but examples of words containing these forty-four sounds (highlighted in bold) are given in Figure 8.1.

Allophones

You must remember when listening to the words listed in Figure 8.1 that the sounds being represented are those that would be made by a speaker with a received pronunciation accent. Even these speakers will not all sound identical: such things as gaps in the teeth can affect the way the sounds are made. In addition, a sound such as /s/ will come out slightly differently depending on the other sounds around it. In pronouncing 'seat' the lips are spread, as if smiling. In 'soon' the lips are rounded. Yet a native speaker will probably be prepared to assert that the gap-toothed speaker, the one saying 'seat' and the one saying 'soon', are all pronouncing the same sound, or phoneme, /s/; the sounds are sufficiently close to come within the same 'segment' of sound in the sound continuum. These variants of /s/ are called allophones.

VOWEL PHONEMES	CONSONANT PHONEMES
m**a**t	**b**all
r**a**ther	**ch**oose
r**are**	**d**aisy
p**aw**	**fl**ower
s**ay**	**g**ate
p**e**t	**h**eat
m**ee**t	**j**am
f**ear**	**k**itchen
f**ir**	**l**amb
l**i**d	**m**atter
p**ie**	**n**ote
h**o**t	cli**ng**
l**oa**n	**p**arcel
p**oo**l	**r**estaurant
f**oo**t	**s**un
m**ou**se	**sh**oes
oil	**t**omato
up	**th**ose
s**ure**	**th**ink
und**er**	**v**ase
	winter
	yacht
	zebra
	illu**si**on

FIGURE 8.1 Phonemes of English.

The sounds of English are differently distributed in other accents. In Lancashire, for instance, the /oo/ sound in 'book' and 'cook' is the same as the /oo/ sound in 'moon' and 'look', and so someone with a Lancashire accent saying 'Look at that cookery book' would make three identical /oo/ sounds in the sentence. The received pronunciation way of sounding the /oo/ in 'book' is used by speakers with a Lancashire accent in 'cup' and 'put'.

Syllables

To break a word into each of its constituent sounds is the most complex way of segmenting it. It is more straightforward to divide words into syllables. A syllable can be defined as the smallest unit of speech that normally occurs in isolation. There are a few vowels, such as 'I', that can exist by themselves, but more usually a syllable consists of a combination of vowel and consonants such as 'hat' or 'pen'. Another way of thinking about syllables is as 'beats' in the rhythm of a word. Children enjoy clapping out the syllables of their names. 'Anne' has one syllable, 'Mary' has two, 'William' has three and so on.

Onsets and rimes

Many groups of syllables share a similar pattern; Figure 8.2 gives examples. In these one-syllable words, the letter or letters that come before the vowel are known as the onset. The rest of the syllable is called the rime. It is considered more helpful for beginner readers to be able to recognise patterns in rimes as in these examples than to launch into decoding a word like 'might' letter by letter. To say /m//i//g//h//t/, or 'tuh' as a child is likely to say, will not act as a useful prompt when decoding this word. If children can recognise 'ight' as a group of letters that occurs in words such as 'sight' and 'fight' and 'might' and 'light', and can remember the sounds they make, they have acquired a useful decoding strategy.

Segmenting words

An experienced reader, when sharing a text with a beginner, must exercise judgement as to how to break the word up to be of most help – syllabically, by onset and rime, or phoneme by phoneme. Only for some of the time will this last option be the same as letter by letter. One of the great difficulties of reading and spelling English words is that, although there are forty-four sounds or phonemes, there are only twenty-six letters of the alphabet. It is obvious then that there can be no straightforward, one-to-one correspondence between sounds and letters.

p	en	s	at	t	ight
m	en	c	at	l	ight
h	en	fl	at	s	ight
t	en	m	at	m	ight

FIGURE 8.2 Syllable patterns.

Graphemes

A grapheme is a written representation of a sound and may consist of one or more letters. Almost all the forty-four English phonemes can be written down in a variety of ways. The sound /b/, for example, is written using one 'b' in 'ball', but in 'rabbit' two 'b's are used. The sound /f/ is written one way in 'flower', another in 'photograph' and differently again in 'enough'. /Sh/ in 'shoes' is different from /sh/ in 'sure'. The sound /k/ can be written as in 'queen' or 'kitten' or 'circus'. The sound we hear in 'pie' looks very different in 'I' and in 'knight'.

Graphs, digraphs, trigraphs

You will have noticed from the above examples that sometimes one letter of the alphabet is used to represent a sound; this is true of the sound /b/ in 'ball' and the sound /p/ in 'pie'. These written symbols are known as graphs (not to be confused with graphs in mathematics). Sometimes two letters of the alphabet combine to represent a sound. Two consonants combine to make the sound /sh/ in 'shine'. Two vowels, 'i' and 'e', combine to make the long /ie/ sound. This means that, although there are only three sounds in 'shine', that is, /sh/ and /ie/ and /n/, there are five letters of the alphabet, because the letters 's' and 'h' combine to make what is called a consonant digraph, and the letters 'i' and 'e' combine to make a vowel digraph. Sometimes three letters of the alphabet, or even four, combine to make one sound. In the word 'knight' the long /ie/ sound is represented by the letters 'i' and 'g' and 'h'. This is called a trigraph. This word has three sounds but six letters because, as well as the trigraph, the sound /n/ at the beginning of the word is represented by a digraph 'kn'.

The English spelling system

The complex correspondences between phonemes and graphemes add up to a very intricate spelling system. There are over 200 rules for combining letters of the alphabet to make the sounds of English. Traditional phonic approaches to reading oversimplify the system by telling children in the early stages that one letter makes one sound: 'a' is for 'apple', 'b' for 'ball', 'c' for 'cat'. Yet it must already be apparent to even four-year-old Amy that 'a' does not make that sound in her name. And how does Christopher account for the way he spells his? Experienced readers very rarely rely on phonic cues alone when deciphering a text because they are the most complex cues of all.

Phonics is frequently mentioned in the media as a reading strategy, but in fact a knowledge of phoneme/grapheme correspondences is just as likely to be needed when writing as when reading. Faced with writing a difficult word with no dictionary available and no one to ask we may resort to trying to break the word down into sounds. This accounts for efforts such as 'skool' or 'becos' in children's writing. No amount of listening to the sounds is ever going to reveal the presence of 'ch' or 'au' in these words. So in this instance, too, phonics is only of partial help, and we must learn to visualise words, as well as listen to them. The more confident children become as readers and writers, using the full range of strategies available, the more we can hope to interest them in the vagaries of the English spelling system. Phonics investigations can play an interesting part in language work at Key Stage 2.

We know from experience that many students find phonology difficult. Yet words are such exciting things that we feel reluctant to leave this chapter with what you may have found to be a dull patch. We want to end therefore with this paean of praise to the word from George Keith and John Shuttleworth (2000: 248):

> In dictionaries, words lie inert but the moment they are put to use they take on new dimensions. There is always something to say about a word once it is in action: its precise, denotative meaning; its connotations; its internal structure or morphology; its sound and rhythm; its appropriateness; its spelling. Even when it is not in use there are always its origins and subsequent history, its family connections, its spelling, its synonyms and antonyms, and statistical frequency to consider. Words are so multidimensional that more than one linguist has been driven to the simplest definition of all of words in writing: i.e., the bits between the spaces. In *A Mouthful of Air*, a very readable book about language, the novelist Anthony Burgess points out that it is only in the Western world that such a priority is given to grammar. In the East words are viewed as much more powerful and well able to take care of themselves.

Whichever way you look at it, the answer to the old question 'What's in a word?' must be 'Far more than the ear can hear and the eye can see'.

Note to activity on page 92

The word 'physical' has seven sounds: /f//i//s//i//c//ə//l/; 'frightened' also has seven: /f//r//i//t//ə//n//d/; and 'transport' has eight: /t//r//a//n//s//p//aw//t/. ə is a symbol known as a schwa in the international phonetic alphabet. It represents the central vowel that can be heard in these words, spoken with a received pronunciation accent.

Summary

In this chapter we have discussed:

- the importance of meeting words in interesting contexts;

- synonyms, connotation and denotation;

- figurative language;

- morphology;

- controlled vocabulary, with particular reference to the Ladybird reading scheme;

- the phonemes (sounds) of English and how words can be segmented into sounds, syllables or onsets and rimes;

- graphemes: the combinations of letters used to write down English sounds.

Activity 4: Audit your word-level knowledge

We've made the point already that in our view developing an enthusiasm for language is your most important task. It is this that will inspire the children you teach. An important part of this is feeling excited about words – not afraid of them, not worried in case you spell them wrongly first time, but keen to explore their meanings, enjoy the sound and the shape of them and experiment with them in your own work. Some of you may have had this enthusiasm since you were children; some may feel that this is the hardest thing of all to achieve. It's very important that you try.

1. Poetry is one of those types of text that many people love but others hate (or think they do). If you are one of the latter, try just for a few minutes reading the following (very brief!) extract from 'The Frozen Man' by Kit Wright (in Harrison and Stuart-Clark 1996: 21), and do your best to find two points about the words he uses that lift the poem above the excitement level of a note to the milkman.

> Out at the edge of town
> where black trees
> crack their
> fingers
> in the icy wind
> and hedges
> freeze
> on their shadows
> and the breath of
> cattle,
> still as boulders
> hangs in rags
> under the rolling moon,
> a man is
> walking alone:

2. The origins of words is something else that you might develop your interest in. Where do you think these words come from?

   (a) chocolate;
   (b) tattoo;
   (c) hubbub;
   (d) lady.

3. In teaching children to read you will need to be confident in your ability to segment words, that is, to split them up in a number of ways. You will learn with experience what kind of segmentation is most helpful to a child on any one occasion. Here are some examples to start you thinking:

   (a) Segmentation into phonemes: Say the word 'bread' aloud. Think carefully about how many sounds you can hear.

(b) Segmentation into onset and rime: Look at and listen to this group of words: bread, head, lead, dead. What do you think would be the most useful 'word splitting' activity to suggest to a child in this case?

(c) Segmentation into morphemes: Look at this group of words: leader, leading, leads, mislead. How might you do the segmenting this time?

(d) Segmentation into syllables: 'Leader' has two syllables (we can clap two beats, as it were); 'leads' has one. Using the children's names is a good way in to some work on syllables. Think of some one-, two- and three-syllable names you might use to practise syllabification.

4. In a previous activity we had 'lead' rhyming with 'dead' and 'head'. However, 'ea' can sound quite different, as in the sentence 'Follow my leader'. The English spelling system is very complex. There is not always a one-to-one correspondence between a sound and the way that sound is written down. To understand more about this, try to think of three other ways of making the vowel sound you can hear after the 'l' in 'leader'.

See pages 166–8 for a commentary on these activities.

Applying language knowledge

9

Applying text-, sentence- and word-level knowledge to fictional texts and poetry

In this chapter and the following three chapters we want to show how the knowledge about language that we have been discussing in the last five chapters can be applied to exploring the meanings of texts that might be found in primary school classrooms. We don't intend to produce materials for direct use in the classroom. There are many books available now that do this, but they assume a degree of language awareness that not all students and teachers have available to them at the moment. Readers may therefore be condemned to following the suggestions on offer without a clear understanding of the underlying language knowledge or of how to adapt the ideas for use with other texts. Our hope is to support teachers in building up their own language knowledge so that they will feel confident in selecting aspects of language work that will usually be text based and planning a variety of interesting activities for their classes drawing on a wide range of texts.

Reading is meaning making

Before we embark on a discussion of any texts, can we remind our readers again of some points we made in Chapter 1. In reading any text, it is not enough to recognise and attach a label to the text structure the writer has chosen, or isolate examples of syntax or vocabulary for comment. In a book written for children, as in any other, we are primarily concerned with making sense of the text and the enjoyment and pleasure that doing this will give us. A good children's book may convey layers of meaning, some of them beyond those immediately accessible to very young readers. To make sense of such a book we draw on some general knowledge, but more particularly we rely on what we as adults know about interpreting texts. In the case of the texts in this chapter, we are drawing on our experience of what fiction and poetry have to offer to a reader who is sensitive to all the texts' possibilities for offering up meaning. Each of us may interpret what we read in a slightly different way, but our readings must be cohesive. That is to say, they must be able to account in a reasonable way for all of the structures, the syntax and the words we have in front of us. In doing this, it is more than likely that we will draw heavily on shared knowledge and memories and, above all, on ways of reading that, if we have been fortunate, we have been taught ourselves and will try to pass on to children.

The Queen's Knickers, Nicholas Allen, Red Fox, 2000

What kind of text is this?

This is a picture book, with words and pictures by the author, that addresses in a very amusing way the question of what the Queen wears underneath her smart coats and dresses. The text introduces us to a number of characters, including the Queen herself and Dilys the maid, who is in charge of the Queen's knickers. Although the book has characters and it is obviously fictional, it is not a story. This is because there is no overall plot; there is no beginning, middle or end. Instead, the book falls into sections, which are described in the next paragraph. Some of the sections are 'mini-narratives'. Occasionally the word 'story' is still used in some classrooms, and by some publishers, as a generic term for almost any kind of reading or writing. In view of the number of text types children are to be introduced to, and to be encouraged to create themselves, it's important to be precise in using the word.

In fact, this text purports to be a report on the subject, although of course a lot of the humour resides in the fact that there never would be any such document. Just to think of it smacks delightfully of lese-majesty. The 'report' characteristics begin immediately with the opening sentence. Instead of a past tense verb, telling of a specific event, which we would expect at the beginning of a story, the author uses a present tense, telling the reader the general state of things: 'The Queen likes to dress smartly.' As reports often do, the text falls into distinct sections:

- Section 1 shows us where the Queen keeps her clothes – in a large wardrobe – and where she keeps her knickers – in a slightly smaller chest of drawers. We meet Dilys the maid and are told that one of her duties is to pack the knickers in a special trunk when the Queen goes away.

- Section 2 is a short narrative section. We know it's narrative because it tells us of a specific event that happened 'one day'. The trunk went missing but happily was found again.

- Section 3 returns us to the reporting present tense. There are some pages of description of knickers for all eventualities.

- Section 4 introduces us to a new character, a little girl, and we meet some first person writing of the 'what if' kind.

From then on the text stays in this more personal mode, with the little girl wondering what knickers the Queen would wear if she visited her school. The blurb on the back of the Red Fox edition of the book suggests that 'Through the eyes of a little girl hoping for a school visit by the Queen, the range of royal underwear is revealed, in all its regal glory.' In fact, it seems to us that this misses the point that there is a sharp contrast between the pseudo-'official' tone of the first three sections, which provides the text with a lot of its humour, and the personal note that is struck at the end.

Sentence and word choices

The sentence structure and vocabulary of some sections of the text are reminiscent of a government document, although a simplified one. It is informative and neutral. One double-page spread is actually labelled 'OFFICIAL H.M. KNICKER GUIDE'. The use of the acronym, the capitalisation and the page layout all reinforce the informative tone. Various pairs of knickers are illustrated and labelled. The connotations of the words on the captions imply some underlying knowledge of the Royal Family: corgis appear on a pair labelled 'At Home', for example, and a plaid pair has the label 'Balmoral (Woollen)'. Another acronym, 'VIP', also requires the reader to bring previous knowledge to bear in order to enjoy the joke. On this occasion the letters refer to 'Very Important Pair'. There are connotations, too, behind the reference to the Christmas knickers, which are 'a gift from Scandinavia'. Another source of humour in the text comes from a double-page spread in which there is a sharp contrast in types of vocabulary: on the first side we find a description of the Royal Knickers, which we are told are 'most valuable' and 'encrusted with diamonds, emeralds and rubies'; on the opposite side of the page we find that they were first worn by Queen Victoria and are 'rather baggy'.

There is no grammatical cohesion linking the last, more personal section with what has gone before. The reader turns the page and encounters a girl sitting at her desk. She is not introduced – in fact we never find out her name. All this leaves space in the text for the readers to create some links for themselves, to tell themselves what they recognise and to speculate on what they would be thinking if they were in the girl's position. In contrast to the first part of the book, the words and pictures now take us 'behind the scenes at the palace' as the little girl imagines the Queen deciding on a new design to be worn on a royal visit to her school. The vocabulary becomes more colloquial: 'there'd be a terrific flap at the palace', 'too frilly . . .', 'too silly . . .', 'I shall just have to . . .' Of course, as we have already said, the fun derives from the fact that none of this could ever happen. The whole text is inviting children to 'think the unthinkable' and the grammatical structure reinforces this with the modal 'would' expressing something that 'might happen if . . .': 'I wonder what knickers the Queen would wear . . .' or 'I would tell her . . .' or the elided form 'There'd be . . .'

Narrative interludes in the text

A personal story

The little girl's 'what if' story is narrated in the first person and contains a lot of direct speech, set out in a conventional way, although only single speech marks are used to demarcate it. Publishers vary in their use of single or double speech marks, and encouraging children to spot the different usages as they go from book to book is one way of drawing their attention to the use of direct speech in text. Another interesting aspect of direct speech is the variety of clues the writer gives to how these words might sound as they come out of people's mouths. This is particularly important if the text is to be read aloud with appropriate intonation and expression. Here we have already been told that there is 'a flap' at the palace and both the Queen and Dilys look very put out. When the Royal Knickermaker is sent for, therefore, the exclamation marks that close each of the Queen's next utterances are a strong clue to Her Majesty's irritated tones. Capitalisation is used again, this time to indicate an even greater degree of royal irritation at the sight of what is considered a most unsuitable design. Another type of clue is employed when the writer tells us that the little girl 'whispered' to Her Majesty.

Environmental print

The book is full of indications to children of how texts of all kinds – captions, labels, posters and so on – fulfil a useful purpose in every aspect of life. A nice example comes at the end of the little girl's story when she imagines a grateful monarch sending her a special note 'by the Royal Mail'. The language structure of the note is suitably lofty in tone. 'Her Majesty wishes to inform you . . . most enjoyable . . . very comfortable.'

A national crisis

To introduce the earlier narrative episode in the book we have been told that Dilys, the maid, has a special trunk to transport the knickers when the Queen goes away. A dramatic note is introduced when the trunk goes missing. The language chosen to tell this story is much more official in tone: 'It caused a great crisis . . .' This time there is only a very small amount of direct speech and instead another convention is used. The words 'The Queen's Knickers! The Queen's Knickers' are depicted coming out of Dilys's mouth, although there is no speech bubble or speech marks. With arms outstretched and mouth wide open, the picture of poor Dilys leaves us in no doubt at all about how these words are to be said. As we expect in narrative, the story is told in the past tense: 'One day, the trunk went missing . . . It caused a great crisis . . . and was only just sorted out . . .' Eventually we discover what had happened to the trunk. As we have just had to do in our text (we wrote 'had happened'), the author then switches to a form of the past tense that enables him to depict events further back in time: 'The trunk had got mixed up with a picnic hamper.'

Reader involvement in the story

Because of the narrative strategies the author uses to tell the story of the trunk's disappearance, there are more opportunities for readers to join in and become 'text creators' themselves. These include:

- information presented in the illustrations rather than in the text;
- a poster depicting the missing 'H.M.'S KNICKER TRUNK';
- police cars and helicopters, clearly labelled, shown rushing about;
- a picture of a large television screen announcing 'NEWS AT TEN'.

There is more evidence of how useful labels are when we visit 'H.R.H. LAUNDRY' and find the puzzled laundry workers unpacking a chicken, bottles of wine and a tin labelled 'Biscuits'. On the washing line behind them, various items of clothing are all carefully labelled with the names of their royal owners.

Punctuation

Learning how to interpret textual conventions is an important part of becoming a reader. An important aspect of this learning concerns the role of punctuation in a text. Twice in *The Queen's Knickers* there are double-page spreads with one line of text underneath each picture. The first example looks like this: 'So she has an enormous wardrobe for her clothes . . .' (left-hand page) and 'and a slightly smaller chest of drawers for all her knickers' (right-hand page). A little further on we find 'It caused a great crisis . . .' followed by 'and was only just sorted out before it reached the NEWS AT TEN'. Traditional reading schemes tended to instil in children the idea that a line of writing is the same as a sentence. It's still not uncommon to find children letting their voices fall and coming to a halt at the right-hand margin, regardless of the punctuation or the sense. The dots are a clear indication here that more is coming and that the sense is not complete.

We have already mentioned that exclamation marks are helpful in indicating how words should be read aloud. Brackets are used for an 'aside' or an 'Oh, and by the way' type of comment.

Graphics

Italics are employed as an indicator of emphasis: examples are 'the trunk went *missing!*', 'was only *just* sorted out' and 'Don't worry about your knickers . . . *no one can see them anyway*'. Bold type is used to enhance the importance of the letter from the Queen, and there are various interesting examples of capitalisation throughout the book providing prominent headings or labels designed to be eye-catching.

In some of what we have said here you will recognise parts of the core learning in literacy in the Primary National Strategy (DCSF 2005) for Year 1 and Year 2. Much of what we have said goes beyond those particular objectives and no one would want to cover all these issues in one series of lesson plans. We have developed them in some detail in the hope that they will shed more light on some of the points we were making in earlier chapters.

Owl Babies, Martin Waddell, illustrated by Patrick Benson, Walker Books, 2006

What kind of text is this?

This text has a classic story structure. It begins by introducing the characters, three baby owls, and we meet them at a specific time and in a particular place in their lives. It's usual to be given extra information about the characters in a story and in this case we learn their names, Sarah and Percy and Bill. This puts the story within a long tradition of anthropomorphised animal stories for children. They are actually 'semi-anthropomorphised'; by this we mean that they have some human characteristics. They have names and they talk to each other, exploring their feelings, and we are told that they think a lot. But they don't wear clothes, drive cars or go for picnics in the way that the more fully anthropomorphised animals in texts such as *The Wind in the Willows* do.

The time is 'Once' and the setting for their story is their house. We have extra information about this too. It's 'a hole in the trunk of a tree' and it has twigs and leaves and owl feathers in it. The illustration on this first page provides the reader with a very close perspective on the owls, so close indeed that readers might feel as if they are peeping into the hole. It is quite obviously night time and very dark. Even before this page is reached, the book's intriguing endpapers have provided the reader with what could be regarded as a very detailed, owls' eye view of the tree, or possibly, if the page is held at arm's length, the patterns could be said to depict an owl with its eyes tight shut. This uncertainty in interpreting the design reminds readers of how similar owls and tree trunks are in colour and markings.

Narrative perspective

The owls live in the tree with the person they call 'Mummy', but who the writer refers to as their 'Owl Mother'. The story is narrated by the author in the third person: we are looking at and listening to the owls. The story is being told about them, not by them. This is emphasised on the second page, when Martin Waddell uses the phrase 'Owl Mother' again: 'One night, they woke up and their Owl Mother was GONE.' After this, we hear each of the baby owls talking about their 'mummy' until 'their Owl Mother' returns on the last page. You might like to consider the connotations you bring to the words 'Owl Mother'. Seen from the readers' perspective they seem to us to hint at an archetypal mother/child relationship, although to Sarah, Percy and Bill she is just their mummy. When the word is used as a title it has a capital 'M', as in 'Where's Mummy?' This is because here it is functioning as a proper noun. When it is referring to one of the group of people who are mothers it has a lower case 'm' (' "I want my mummy," said Bill') because it is being used as a common noun. Other nouns that can belong in both classes are president, queen, princess: 'The president is the head of state' but 'The building was inaugurated by President Clinton'.

Plot structure

Once the characters have been introduced and their setting established, the main problem that the story explores is, interestingly, a psychological one: the baby owls' fear of being left alone in the dark. There are no villains in this story, nothing comes to threaten the owls, and as we hinted in the last paragraph they are actually very much at home in their habitat and well camouflaged. Nature has equipped owls to be most at home in the dark. But, the author suggests, as yet they don't feel safe, for exactly the same reasons as for many of the child readers of this story. The night seems very black, and very big, and full of movement. The illustrations are highly successful in depicting the owls' feelings of vulnerability. Patrick Benson manages to convey an amazing variety of expressions on owl faces.

Characters

To study the characters is often one of the main pleasures of reading a story, and it is particularly important in this story because of the absence of events. Everything hinges around how each of the owls copes with the situations they find themselves in. Writers have a variety of means of depicting character. Readers are sometimes told about them directly, by the author, or can form judgements about them from what other characters say. What they do is also very revealing. More than anything in this story, it is what they say, the words that the writer puts into their mouths, that reveal their personalities. A pattern is established whereby, almost always, when one speaks all the owls speak, always in the same order, oldest to youngest. This makes them seem 'an entity'; they are the 'owl babies'. Interestingly, the title of the book has no definite article: 'Owl Babies' hints at the generic, rather than the specific, in the same way that we suggested 'Owl Mother' seemed to represent a type, rather than a particular one.

Sometimes writers will go to some lengths to find variants of 'said'. In this text, apart from setting the ball rolling with ' "Where's Mummy?" asked Sarah', almost all the other examples of direct speech are followed by 'said'. This has the effect of emphasising the fact that they spoke 'as members of a team', and also perhaps that they were feeling very subdued.

Sarah's role, as befits the eldest, is to draw attention to the problem in the first place, then to suggest possible reasons for it, and to offer comfort to the others, and hope. When hope seems dead, she's the first to voice their fears. Percy, who has that difficult position in any family, the middle child, largely reacts to what Sarah says, and Bill, the baby, says the same thing throughout: 'I want my mummy.' In trying to offer comfort, Sarah suggests: 'She'll bring us mice and things that are nice.' The rhyme here, and the word order, are strongly reminiscent of lines from a nursery rhyme, such as 'Sugar and spice, and all things nice . . .' The unspoken assumption is that Sarah is valiantly trying to 'play mummy' at this point and to remind her brothers of something they have shared with their mother. She is only partially successful, as the choice of words for Percy's rejoinder, 'I suppose so!', makes clear.

Interestingly, the one occasion when Percy seems to be more than just an echo of Sarah is when, for the first time, she voices her fears: 'Suppose she got lost.' This seems to free him to say what's on his mind too and his idea is even more dramatic than Sarah's – a fox might have got her. This all seems so dreadful that the baby owls 'shut down all systems', close their eyes and just endure. And at this point their mother returns, coming from behind them, so that we have a back view of them too, enduring on their branch. Alliteration heightens the effect: 'Soft and silent, she swooped through the trees . . .' It's interesting to consider your response to these words. In other contexts we might have interpreted the words with their repeated 's' sounds as sinister or threatening, yet here we read them as expressions of motherly love.

When the baby owls see her, the unvaried repetitions of 'said' are abandoned: ' "Mummy," they cried.' This is the time to switch to action, and the verbs are of the bold variety we have referred to in an earlier chapter. They 'flapped' and they 'danced' and they 'bounced'. Their mother is not given very many words, but what she says is a very typically 'motherly' thing: 'WHAT'S ALL THE FUSS? . . . You knew I'd come back.'

Some characteristics of speech

A close look at the words that come out of the mouths of the baby owls reminds the reader that people frequently don't speak in complete sentences. Often they complete a previous speaker's sentences, as Percy does when, after Sarah has said, 'I think she's gone hunting', he adds, 'To get us our food!' Or they add a comment of their own to what a previous speaker has said. Here is Percy again, this time adding to Sarah's 'She'll be back' with his comment, 'Back soon!'

Sentences frequently begin with 'and' or 'but', including one of the most important sentences in the whole book, so important that it is written on a page by itself, in capital letters: 'AND SHE CAME.' Beginning sentences with 'and' and 'but' is an issue of usage, rather than of grammar. Interestingly, we have found that people who claim to be totally ignorant of grammar are still very much exercised by these 'rules of usage'. They seem to remember nothing from school about nouns, verbs, subordinate clauses and so on, but branded on their memory are rules of usage, such as these, or the one about never splitting an infinitive (as in *Star Trek's* opening sequence: 'To boldly go . . .'). David Crystal tells a story of how once, after presenting a radio programme, he got a letter that said, 'Children who split infinitives are much more likely to go around breaking shop windows'. You may well have strong views of your own on this subject, but you need to be aware that you will find 'ands' and 'buts' starting sentences in some of the most beautiful prose and poetry in English. And increasingly you will find split infinitives too.

Punctuation

As in *The Queen's Knickers*, a sentence in a bracket is used for an aside: '(all owls think a lot)'. It's a comment that is repeated several times throughout the book, so it's hard to ignore. It reminds readers of the place owls have in our culture and mythology, as symbols of wisdom, the emblem of Athena, goddess of Wisdom.

Speech marks in this text are of the double variety.

Exclamation marks are frequently used to reinforce the owls' feelings of fear and dismay, and, as in *The Queen's Knickers*, words in italics also heighten these feelings or add emphasis: ' "I think we should all sit on *my* branch," said Sarah.' One of the most vivid uses of italics is in the sentence 'It was dark in the wood and they had to be brave, for things *moved* all around them.' This sinister sentence is brilliantly supported by the illustration, which shows a very large, dark wood and three very tiny owls. Our perspective as readers is from some distance away, in the wood. However closely we look, we can see nothing that might be moving other than leaves or grasses. But if we stop and think about this, and allow ourselves to empathise with the owls, we may remember how sinister the rustling of leaves and grass can sound in the dark. This is another example of sparseness of text working more dramatically than too much writing. Readers are well able to supply some ideas for themselves, thus drawing them in to the story.

The Queen's Knickers is an amusing text, working entirely on a surface level. We may enjoy going back to it again and again, but we are very unlikely to read any more into it on subsequent re-readings. It is none the worse for that. *Owl Babies*, on the other hand, is one of those books that, although written with children in mind, will continue to have significance for its readers long after they have conquered their fear of the dark.

'The Frozen Man', Kit Wright, in *A Year Full of Poems*, edited by Michael Harrison and Christopher Stuart-Clark, Oxford University Press, 1996

What kind of text is this?

Because of the layout (see Figure 9.1), the text works visually as well as verbally to create an image of a winding path on the page. Much of the poem's drama comes from the contrast that the poet establishes between two settings, one hostile, one welcoming. The 'frozen man' of the title is making his way from one to the other. Apart from the title, in which the word 'frozen' arouses images in the mind of the reader of extreme cold, or even of somebody in whom life is temporarily suspended, we are told no more about the man until the setting he is travelling through has been well established. It's a cold and lonely one. There are no signs of human habitation, and very little movement of any kind on the ground except the stiff crackling of frozen branches in the wind. In contrast to this darkness and stillness, the moon rolls overhead. The man is alone. The text layout chosen by the poet enables him to put the word on a line by itself, which gives it extra significance.

The man seems to be pushing along at a fairly rapid rate because his footsteps ring on the road. The short lines, too, seem to suggest quick movement. In today's world particularly, a man walking along a lonely road at night could suggest to some readers that he is up to no good. But as we read on, the evidence suggests that there is no danger here. The poet carefully places the readers with himself, 'Here', in the much more friendly setting of a warm house in the heart of town. We are told that we can 'hear' the warmth – an unusual word to choose perhaps, but this is a live fire, burning in the hearth. This is the very house that the frozen man is aiming for. We realise that he represents no threat when we reach the last three lines of the poem: the imperative is used not just once but three times to urge strongly the readers to let him in. The mystery remains of who is the owner of the house, who the lonely man is and what the connection is between them. It's made very clear by the poet that the heart of town is the place to be on such a night. The countryside in contrast is cold and unwelcoming. This reverses the idea we often find in stories and poems of the hot and dusty town as a place to escape from into the fresh air of woods and fields.

Out at the edge of town where
black trees
crack their fingers in the
icy wind
and hedges freeze on their
shadows
and the breath of cattle, still as
boulders
hangs in rags
under the rolling moon,
a man is walking alone:
on the coal-black road his cold
feet
ring
and
ring.
Here in a snug house at the
heart of town
the fire is burning
red and yellow and gold:
you can hear the warmth like a
sleeping cat
breathe softly
in every room.
When the frozen man comes
to the door,
let him in,
let him in,
let him in.

FIGURE 9.1 'The Frozen Man' by Kit Wright.

Sentences

The poem consists of three sentences: one is used to establish the scene in the countryside, one in the town and the third to give the order to let the man in. The first two are deliberately contrasted with parallel words to open each sentence: 'Out at the edge of town' and 'Here . . . at the heart of town'.

In the first sentence, the hostile environment is established in a series of relative clauses that accumulate in the readers' minds to create a picture of something a person would want to move briskly through and out of. There are three of these clauses:

- 'where black trees crack their fingers in the icy wind';
- 'hedges freeze on their shadows';
- 'the breath of cattle, still as boulders, hangs in rags under the rolling moon'.

110

The sense of these images piling up one on top of the other is reinforced by the use of 'and' to link each one of them to the one that has gone before. Grammatically, one of these 'ands' is redundant, but would the description of the night's conditions be the same without it? There is a similar use of 'and' for emphasis, especially as the word gets a line to itself, in

> his cold
> > feet
> > ring
> > > and
> > > ring.

There's a less hurried tone in the second sentence. No one is hurrying away from the warmth and glow of the fire. The sentence is constructed in such a way that emphasis falls heavily on the main clause: 'the fire is burning red and yellow and gold'.

Punctuation

Both the first and second sentences make use of colons (:). Colons have an anticipatory effect; they lead the reader on from what precedes to what follows. They seem to be very suitable punctuation marks therefore in the context of this poem. Colons can have several uses. In both cases in this text they seem to point to the relationship between one clause and another; they keep us moving along the road, as it were, without the halt that a full stop would bring about. When the full stop does come, after 'room', as we wait for the frozen man to arrive and knock on the door, the stronger pause seems all the more dramatic.

Word choice

The meanings we have been suggesting at text and sentence level seem to be reinforced at the word level. The sounds of words are frequently important in reinforcing their sense. In the cold first half of the poem we find the internal rhyme of 'black' with 'crack' – cold, hard sounds. In the second half, the sounds are of the murmuring and hissing of the fire: 'warmth' and 'breathe', 'sleeping' and 'softly'. Colours too provide strong contrasts: 'black', 'shadows' and 'coal-black' contrasting with 'red' and 'yellow' and 'gold'.

Figurative language

There is a ghostly, other-worldly feeling about the countryside. This comes partly from the author's treatment of the trees: they are personified, cracking their fingers in the icy wind. The cattle's breath adds to the ghostly effect, 'hanging in rags', while the cattle themselves seem more dead than alive, standing 'still as boulders'. Over all this we imagine the moon casting an unearthly light. The words used to describe the house all have living, breathing connotations. The house is at the 'heart' of town, for example. Consider the possible synonyms for this word, and what their effects might have been. The centre of town? The middle of town? The idea of the heartbeat is picked up by the description of the warmth from the fire, which can be heard breathing softly. The simile used is 'like a sleeping cat', a reference that usually carries overtones of peaceful domesticity. The house is 'snug', a word that has strong connotations of warmth and cosiness.

Each reader will bring different images to this scene. It can be understood on a literal level, as someone coming home after travelling, or after work perhaps. On the other hand, it is possible to see the whole poem as an extended metaphor, a plea for forgiveness, perhaps, from someone who has been 'out in the cold'. Reading is a matter of personal interpretation of the evidence in the text. This particular text allows for some freedom of interpretation.

Harry Potter and the Philosopher's Stone, J.K. Rowling, Bloomsbury, 1997

What kind of text is this?

The novel is largely set in a fantasy world that exists alongside the world most of us live in, but in another dimension. It helps to appreciate its humour if readers can bring to it experience of reading other kinds of narrative texts, especially traditional school stories of the 'Jennings' variety. This is because many of the features of a boarding school story are to be found here, but humorously adapted to a magical dimension. For example, Harry Potter goes off to Hogwarts School of Witchcraft and Wizardry on the school train, which leaves Kings Cross from Platform 9¾. He has spent some time in London getting his school uniform and his kit together, but these consist of items such as three sets of plain work robes (black); one plain pointed hat (black) for day wear; one pair of protective gloves (dragon hide or similar); one wand; one cauldron (pewter, standard size 2). The exotic details and the mundane sit amusingly side by side. New pupils are told, for example, that 'all pupils' clothes should carry name tags' (p. 52). There are bossy prefects and nervous first years on the school train. There are school rules: pupils may have pets, but they must be owls or cats or toads. No first years are allowed their own broomsticks.

Creating an imaginary world

We can accept this imaginary world because it is presented to us with a convincing completeness. It has a social and political order. For example, there is a Ministry of Magic whose job it is to make sure that Muggles, which is the name given to non-wizards, never find out about the magical dimension. It has a history and flora and fauna. We know something about these from the titles of the books Harry has to have for school, and from the books in the school library. They have titles such as *A History of Magic* by Bathilda Bagshot and *One Thousand Magical Herbs and Fungi* by Phyllida Spore. It has a bank – Gringotts – run by goblins, with vaults that go deep under London, and its own monetary system.

The central character

It's not just memories of school stories that come to mind when reading this book. The plot provides powerful resonances of many other kinds of text. As in so much children's fiction, Harry Potter is an orphan. His parents have been killed by the arch villain, Voldemort, who is still around and very much a threat to Harry himself. Harry is brought up by a Muggle aunt and uncle, who treat him cruelly and try to prevent him from finding out that he is a wizard. Readers know about Harry's latent powers, although he is kept in ignorance, and therefore wait with interest to see how he will be rescued from his miserable Muggle existence.

At Hogwarts School of Witchcraft and Wizardry, although he knows by now that he has an important destiny, Harry feels weak and threatened by both bullying pupils and powerful professors, one of whom, at least, appears to hate him. As in many a good fairy story, however, when he meets the many tribulations that come his way he is given powerful aids: faithful friends, a 'cloak of invisibility', and, best of all, because he turns out to be good at Quidditch, the school game, he acquires a powerful broomstick, a 'Nimbus 2000'.

His final encounters with the powers of evil are reminiscent of legend or of Greek mythology. He first meets his enemies in an enchanted forest but doesn't recognise them for what they are. He is helped on that occasion by centaurs who live in the forest. The climax of the struggle comes after a series of trials reminiscent of the labours of Hercules, deep in the underground labyrinthine cellars of the school. One of the memorable things about the text is the way it can switch from tongue-in-cheek humour, like the spectacle of a dragon's egg hatching, to the gruesomeness of the arch villain, Voldemort, drinking the blood of a dead unicorn.

The importance of names

The characters include the Dursleys, Harry's aunt, uncle and cousin, who are the most Muggle of all Muggles; Albus Dumbledore, the head at Hogwarts; among Harry's school friends the swot Hermione; and the school bully Malfoy and his henchmen Crabbe and Goyle. There is a taciturn school caretaker called Filch; Hagrid, the faithful retainer with a rather murky past; and, of course, the evil Voldemort himself. The author is clearly very much alive to the power of names. The names possess the characteristics of those who own them. It's not surprising therefore that she makes 'Voldemort' a name that only the truly brave can bring themselves to utter; to others he is known as 'You-Know-Who' or 'He-Who-Must-Not-Be-Named'.

Settings

The prosaic and the magical also sit side by side in the descriptions of the settings. For example, the train ride to Hogwarts could have been straight out of any school story, although with some interesting additions. Yet the first sight of the school is from another genre altogether. The pupils walk down a steep, narrow path and arrive at the edge of a great black lake. They round a bend and 'Perched atop a high mountain on the other side, its windows sparkling in the starry sky, was a vast castle with many turrets and towers'. They are ordered into a fleet of little boats and 'moved off all at once, gliding across the lake which was as smooth as glass'. These are words and images from a story of King Arthur, and yet a few seconds later Hagrid is shouting 'Heads down!' and 'Oy, you there! Is this your toad?' before returning readers to the magical by knocking three times on the castle door (pp. 83–4).

Issues at word level

Homophones

A lot of the richness of this book is at the text and the word level. The name J.K. Rowling chooses for ordinary, non-magical mortals, 'Muggles', is possibly a homophone for 'Muddles'. Homophones are words that sound the same but have a different meaning or a different spelling. More mundane examples include 'tale' and 'tail' or 'bred' and 'bread'.

Playing with words

We have already referred to the fairytale nuances of the text. One aspect of this is a magic mirror known as 'The Mirror of Erised'. The name is a mirror image of 'desire'. The mirror shows those who look into it what they most desire.

The emotional impact of sounds

The phonology or sound system of English is exploited in the text, often in the names chosen for characters or places. Sounds are not neutral; those hearing them associate them with particular qualities and attributes, as we described when discussing accents in Chapter 6 (p. 53). Hogwarts School has four houses and their names immediately convey to native English speakers something of the qualities of each house: they are Hufflepuff, Ravenclaw, Slytherin and Gryffindor. Could Harry, the noble hero of this tale, have been in Hufflepuff? It seems unthinkable. As these word associations are an important part of the way meaning is made in this book, one wonders how differently the text is read in America, where it has had great success though under a different title, *Harry Potter and The Sorcerer's Stone*. In an interview for an American magazine, Joanne Rowling says that she enjoyed editing the book for the American version: 'The differences between "British English" (of which there must be at least 200 versions) and "American English" (ditto!) are a source of constant interest and amusement to me.'

The book is too long and too full of language richness to discuss it all in detail, but we would like to take a look at one episode more closely.

A closer look at one episode at text, sentence and word level

Text

The extract we have chosen is in Chapter 10. Harry Potter has shown remarkable prowess on a broomstick, and so against all the Hogwarts traditions he has been chosen to play Quidditch for his house, Gryffindor. He has no knowledge of the game at all and so is to be given some private coaching by Wood, the house Quidditch captain.

One of the difficulties for authors of inventing worlds is that readers can inevitably bring no previous experience of any kind to bear in reacting to them. The author has to work hard therefore to build belief. If the game in question was rugby, or croquet, it would bring with it lots of associations, though not necessarily the same ones of course for all readers. Quidditch, we are told, has a long and honourable history. We know this because books have been written about it, such as *Quidditch Through the Ages*, and traditions have grown up around it, such as that first years don't usually play. We know that it is a great honour to play for the house. In this way, the author links our ideas of the game to what we might know about rugby, lacrosse or other sports with a long school tradition.

Figurative language

Another difficulty is that no reader will have the slightest idea of how to play the game, and yet it is important for the plot that some of the rules at least are understood. One way of explaining how to play would be to compare the game to something else. Yet again, in an invented world, similes and comparisons of all kinds can be difficult. How can characters who don't live in the 'real' world make such comparisons, or understand them? The author is helped here by the fact that Harry Potter was brought up as a Muggle, although Wood was not. This allows her to put a comparison into Harry's mind. She tells us that 'At either end of the pitch were three golden poles with hoops on the end. They reminded Harry of the little plastic sticks Muggle children blew bubbles through, except that these were fifty feet high' (p. 123). Later on, though, when Harry tries to use basketball as a simile for Quidditch, 'That's sort of like basketball on broomsticks with six hoops' (p. 124), Wood doesn't understand, and Harry quickly drops the point (though the readers will have been enlightened by the comparison).

Sentences

We are also helped to learn the rules of Quidditch because Harry himself is very ignorant, but very keen to learn. The author has him hanging on to Wood's every word, and repeating everything Wood tells him, which gives readers ample opportunity to learn alongside him. Wood is also trying to make his speech as clear as he possibly can as befits someone who is trying to teach the rules of a game to a beginner (p. 124).

'This ball's called the Quaffle,' said Wood. 'The Chasers throw the Quaffle to each other and try to get it through one of the hoops to score a goal. Ten points every time the Quaffle goes through one of the hoops. Follow me?'

'The Chasers throw the Quaffle and put it through the hoops to score,' Harry recited.

Words

The passage above has lots of invented words for readers to remember, such as 'Quaffle'. Later on in the same passage (p. 124) Rowling refers to 'Bludgers' and 'Snitch'. One is tempted on first reading it to wonder whether the author couldn't have done better here. The words really do sound rather stupid. And then one remembers the words of Il Duce to his son-in-law in *Captain Corelli's Mandolin* by Louis de Bernières (1994: 14): 'Been playing golf? I thought so . . . I wish I had time for it myself. One feels so much at sea when talk turns to mashie-niblicks, cleeks and mid-irons.'

Though there's a lot to remember, there are sufficient similarities with more traditional games to prevent readers feeling totally lost. And then, just when we feel on fairly familiar ground, the writer throws in a totally outrageous point: 'A game of Quidditch only ends when the Snitch is caught, so it can go on for ages – I think the record is three months, so they had to keep bringing on substitutes so the players could get some sleep.'

The comments we have made on these four books arise of course from our own readings of them. By now you should be sufficiently familiar with what we have been saying about the processes of reading not to be surprised if your reading of these texts is different from ours. We hope that we have grounded our readings sufficiently in the linguistic evidence we had in front of us, but our understanding of that evidence, the meanings, and hence the enjoyment that we take from each text, are to a large extent a matter of our own histories as readers and as native English speakers.

Summary

In this chapter we have discussed how to apply text-, sentence- and word-level knowledge to:

- *The Queen's Knickers* by Nicholas Allen;

- *Owl Babies* by Martin Waddell;

- 'The Frozen Man' by Kit Wright;

- *Harry Potter and the Philosopher's Stone* by J.K. Rowling.

10

Applying text-, sentence- and word-level knowledge to non-fiction texts

Splish, Splash, Splosh! A Book about Water, Mick Manning and Brita Granström, Franklin Watts, 2004

What kind of text is this?

This is an 'explanation' type of text, giving an account of the processes involved in the water cycle, but constructed in such a way as to make the information very accessible and interesting for Key Stage 1 readers. This is achieved partly because of the illustrations that occupy half of each double-page spread. A small boy and his dog are shown taking part themselves in each stage of the cycle. Sometimes, as when, for example, the writers start the account on the beach, or when the water reaches the stage of being piped into and out of homes, the boy and his dog are seen against a background of everyday life going on around them. At other times, as they are whisked out into the deep ocean on a dolphin's back, or sail high in the sky on a cloud, they have left the everyday world of mothers, sisters, shopping and other mundane occupations far behind them. Because it is an explanation of a process, as water is sucked from the sea only to return to it eventually as rain, it makes sense to read the book from the beginning. There is no index or contents page, encouraging readers to jump in at an intermediate point, although there is a glossary with page references.

This book is ideal for sharing with an adult or more experienced reader because there is so much to talk about in the illustrations, in the text itself and in the diagrams that support and reinforce the words.

The structure of the text

It is usual for an explanation text to open with a general statement to introduce the topic and then for each statement to be linked in a series of logical steps, perhaps using sequencing words such as 'next' or 'then'. Instead, each double-page spread starts with the words

- 'Splish, Splash, Splosh'.

This enables even an inexperienced reader to join in the reading and have some fun. The sounds of the words are a constant reminder that it is water that we are thinking about. The writers are in no hurry to get on to a 'next' or 'then' stage. Readers are free to take the explanations at their own pace and are encouraged to daydream and to wonder as well as to learn.

As the text starts, we find ourselves on the beach with the boy and his dog. There is no introductory statement. Instead, after reminding readers of what they have observed waves doing on the beach, they are faced with the question that is to be pursued through the rest of the book: 'Where do they come from and where do they go?'

We are shown scenes that we are probably familiar with – waves coming gently and gracefully into shore, slapping against boats and jetties – and then, as the boy sweeps out to sea on the dolphin's back, we sail off into the more unfamiliar and exotic parts of the water cycle. The facts are conveyed in memorable word pictures:

- We find out, for example, that parts of the sea are so deep that huge mountain ranges can lie under the surface.

- We are encouraged to envisage sea water splashing over dolphins' backs and between sharks' teeth.

- On another occasion, when the water cycle reaches the sewage stage, we discover how bath water mixes with other waste water and runs along sewer tunnels, and we are shown a cutaway view of a typical high street. While shoppers go about their business, not very far beneath their feet rats and an alligator paddle in the sewer and we learn that unwanted pets are found there having been flushed down the toilet!

The writers' stance towards the readers

Initially, the writers adopt an impersonal, informative tone, but as the text reaches the domestic water stages they address the readers directly, reminding them that they are part of the process and have a role in ensuring that nothing goes wrong with it: 'Then it joins the mains water supply to your house! . . . You have a wash . . .' and, finally, 'We have to be very careful and keep water clean . . .'

Graphic conventions

The text is laid out in interesting ways, with one typeface for the stages of the water cycle and another for incidental but related pieces of information. Sometimes text is laid across a page in waves or following the contours of a rainbow. Diagrams are clearly labelled and provide a valuable support to the text.

Sentence structure

In one or two places we think the syntactic pattern chosen might confuse inexperienced readers. Subjects of sentences have been in the plural:

- waves;
- clouds;
- raindrops;
- streams.

Then the sentence pattern changes:

- 'Streams rush headlong into a crazy waterfall, that crashes into a river . . . and fills up a dam.'

Then we are given more information about 'the' dam. To the experienced reader, this use of the singular represents waterfalls, rivers and dams in general. To a young reader, the impression might well be given that there is only one of each.

Word choices

The vocabulary helps considerably to make the text appealing to younger readers. The words chosen are more colourful than those usually employed to describe a scientific process. Sometimes they have an onomatopoeic quality:

- waves 'slop' under boats and 'slap' against harbours and jetties;
- sea water 'washes' over dolphins' backs and 'slips' through shipwrecks.

  Almost all the verbs attract the reader's attention:

- waves 'come roaring in';
- raindrops 'burst from the clouds';
- clouds 'swirl into a storm';
- monsoons can 'destroy buildings and flood towns'.

  Adjectives too are vivid: rainwater is 'wild' and 'muddy'; in the sewers, waste water becomes 'thick and sludgy'.

Figurative language

Both metaphors and similes are found in the text. We are told that waves 'dance', waterfalls are 'crazy' and water 'splutters'. Clouds come sailing inland, like ships.

Technical terms

In spite of the quite poetic quality of the writing, there is plenty of information available and readers are introduced to terms such as 'chlorine', 'reservoir', 'evaporation', 'filter' and 'U-bend', in addition to the ones we have already mentioned.

It isn't easy to present accurate scientific information in such a way as to hold the interest and attention of young, inexperienced readers. In this book, words, pictures and diagrams work together admirably in an original mixture to achieve this. It would be interesting to discuss both this text and the others we will consider in this chapter, even with readers at Key Stage 2, as examples of the different ways in which it is possible to construct non-fiction texts.

Spider Watching, Vivian French, illustrated by Alison Wisenfeld, Walker Books, 1996

What kind of text is this?

The blurb on the front and back covers of this book gives an inkling of one aspect of the writer's intention: to persuade readers to overcome any prejudice they may have towards spiders. 'Learn to love spiders', readers are urged, and 'cousin Helen hated spiders – until she looked more closely at their webs and saw what clever, interesting creatures they are . . .'

Text layout

The book is structured ingeniously to achieve its aim of showing children that spiders are harmless, interesting and, in this country at least, nothing to be afraid of. The right-hand side of each double-page spread consists of a narrative; the left-hand page provides the scientific information. Thus the emotional appeal of a story can be reinforced by revelations from natural history. The book is not difficult or confusing to read, especially as each side is printed using a different font. Readers are reminded in the index to look for words they are interested in, in both typefaces.

Narrative sections: plot and characters

On the narrative side, although the plot is simple, the story is effective. This is no crude use of narrative simply to 'sugar the scientific pill'. The action revolves around the writer's memory of a childhood visit made by her cousin, Helen. The story is told by Vivian French in the first person. Helen hated spiders, whereas the author and her brother were very fond of them. As the story goes on, Helen's feelings and attitudes change and develop. We have evidence for this from the things she does and from what she says. For example, she is prepared to handle a spider, and pleads with the children's mother not to sweep all the spiders out of the shed.

This change of heart is really no thanks to the author's brother, who is cast in the role of 'technical expert'. He puts Helen right in a rather superior way whenever she exaggerates or makes inaccurate statements. We are told by his sister that this was 'part of his character'. She says, 'My brother liked people to get things right.' He is keen on telling his cousin all the gory bits of information, and pushes her to take the next step before she is quite ready for it.

The narrator comes across clearly as a more diplomatic character. She seems to be looking for ways of starting the change process in her cousin, beginning by drawing Helen's attention to the beauty of a web. Helen feels guilty when she accidentally damages it and takes her first step towards admiring spiders instead of fearing them when she sees how the web is mended. The narrator seems to sense that a significant step has been made, and takes everyone off for breakfast.

The next move is to offer to show Helen a web, and again Helen is overcome with guilt when it is discovered that the children's mother is about to placate her guest by sweeping all the spiders out of the shed. Helen becomes a 'spider defender' and from there, swiftly, a spider lover. Plot and characters, then, two of the staples of story structure, have been handled in a subtle way in a relatively short space. No criticism has been made of Helen, although her fear has been shown to be unnecessary. The point has also been made that the subject of spiders has enough in it to interest all kinds of people – the gentle and the more bloodthirsty.

Structuring the information

The non-narrative text is skilfully linked to the story. As we become involved in the feelings of each of the three main characters, issues are thrown up that are explored on each parallel page (see Figure 10.1).

This does mean of course that the more piecemeal approach that we characterised in Chapter 5 as being typical of reading non-fiction is not appropriate here. It is not the readers' questions that are being addressed so much as Helen's, and so the facts are read in the order that the narrative determines. An index is provided, but it seems to us that this would be used only after a first reading of the book from cover to cover, if readers wanted to go back and refresh their minds about a point they remembered.

The non-fiction text also supports the fiction in trying to enlist admiration and respect for the spiders. In this case it is achieved by reminding readers of the similarities between spiders and ourselves; both species spin, mend and catch their food.

Sentences

At the sentence level, the book offers a good opportunity to compare the narrative past tense with the report style's continuous present. The two opening sentences are:

- 'My brother loved spiders, and so did I.'
- 'House spiders are some of the most common types of spider.'

The report is written in scientific, though very accessible, prose. The subjects of the sentences are 'spiders' in general, or 'an average house spider' or 'a spider' or 'the spider' used in a general sense. One sentence tells us 'There are more than thirty thousand kinds'. This use of 'there' is known to linguists as an 'existential there'. In other words it tells us that something exists, in contrast to the use of the word in a

House spiders can be found in the shed of the house where Helen is staying	⟷	House spiders are among the most common types of spider
House spiders haven't got hundreds of horrid hairy legs as Helen thinks	⟷	What does a spider look like upside down through a magnifying glass?
Spiders are not 'horrible insects' as Helen says	⟷	What group of animals do spiders belong to?
Helen is shown a web in the garden	⟷	How do spiders make their webs?

FIGURE 10.1 Narrative and non-narrative links in 'Spider Watching'.

sentence such as 'She lives over there.' Its use suggests that some new information is going to be offered.

In keeping with its scientific tone, spiders are not anthropomorphised at all in this text, except perhaps on one occasion when we are told that 'they don't like holes in their webs'. We're not sure whether it's a scientific fact that spiders have feelings, but we very much doubt it. No metaphors or similes are used in talking about them. Two sentences stand out as different from the rest. They are used to make a direct address to the reader. In the imperative mood, the writer urges the readers:

- 'Save a spider . . . place a towel over the side of the bath.'

The second example is:

- 'But if you pick one up, handle it very carefully.'

As we might expect, there are many more signs of personal involvement in the narrative syntax. The subject of the sentences is often 'Helen'. Otherwise, they almost all contain a pronoun and/or a determiner:

- 'My brother and I';
- 'we';
- 'our cousin';
- 'our mum'.

Words

The contrast between the scientific prose and the narrative is marked at the word level too. The narrative places huge emphasis on feelings. We are told about these in two ways. There are many occasions when feelings are mentioned directly:

- 'my brother and I loved';
- 'we were very proud';
- 'she screamed and screamed';

- ■ 'she hated';
- ■ 'my brother liked';
- ■ 'I'm not afraid';
- ■ 'you squealed';
- ■ 'she loved it'.

This last example brings the story to a very successful conclusion because it marks Helen's arrival at the point where her cousins were when the story started. Before we reach that point, however, we have also had a good many indirect expressions of feeling. Amongst these are:

- ■ 'she made us' [keep the back door shut];
- ■ 'we had to' [go and play in the garden];
- ■ 'I didn't mean to' [damage the spider's web];
- ■ 'my brother snorted' [at something Helen said].

There is a very slightly more sentimental treatment of the spiders in this text, particularly at the point where it's feared they might have all been swept away: ' "Poor little spiders," she said. "Are they all dead?" ' Thankfully they are not. We are told: 'At least seven or eight spiders were already tiptoeing out. They scuttled up into the corners.'

The vocabulary of the scientific text is much more restrained:

- ■ 'An average house spider won't live much longer than . . .';
- ■ 'Spiders are protected by . . .';
- ■ 'Spiders belong to . . .'

There are plenty of technical terms for parts of a spider's anatomy, and for different members of the arachnid family: 'palps', 'fangs', 'spinnerets' and 'tailed whip scorpion' are some examples. As we have said before in an earlier chapter, there is no reason why young children would be put off by these terms. They may not remember them, or be able to spell them, but they will find them fascinating.

An interesting opportunity to compare the fictional treatment of the subject with the scientific comes when the brother indulges in some teasing of his cousin:

- ■ 'He tried to frighten her by telling her how they suck the juices from flies and other things they catch.'

The scientific prose explains this rather gruesome process in a very matter of fact way:

- ■ 'Spiders can only eat liquid food. They stun their prey with their fangs, then inject a special juice into the body. This turns the insides soft enough for the spider to suck out.'

(It is at this point that readers are reminded that we also catch our food.)

Pirate Diary. The Journal of Jake Carpenter, Richard Platt, illustrated by Chris Riddell, Walker Books, 2003

What kind of text is this?

The title indicates that the text purports to be a diary, and the blurb on the back of the book informs us that the diary starts on 23 September 1716 and that its writer is Jake Carpenter, who is nine years old. So as we would expect, the book is written in the first person, it is organised chronologically and each entry is dated. However, the entries are all written in complete sentences and there is far too much detail for this text to sound like a genuine diary. Jake would have had neither the time nor, probably, the inclination to write as much as this – and how do we account for all the vivid full-colour illustrations? This would be an interesting point to discuss with children: here we have a text masquerading as an example of one type of text and having some of its features, but what else could it be classified as?

To many children the book will read like a story. It has a plot, of sorts, with a 'once upon a time' style of beginning, a middle with a crisis (or several!) and a 'happy ever after' end. There are also some very interesting characters. But in the bookshop it is shelved alongside non-fiction texts. It is, as the *Sunday Times* reviewer called it, 'A fabulously illustrated ripping yarn that is also . . . non-fiction.' It has been carefully researched and the author obviously wanted children to learn from, as well as be amused by, the text. This is clear from the information that is provided on a wide range of topics, including:

- navigational issues;
- whales and carvings made from whales' teeth;
- mermaids;
- knots – and how the lives of everyone on board a ship can depend on them at times;
- burials at sea.

It's worth pointing out to children that the author and illustrator list their sources on page 64 and they emphasise that they 'are especially grateful', because they searched in more than forty books for details that would make the text and pictures of *Pirate Diary* authentic.

A child would want to read the book, at least initially, from the beginning to the end, although there are a detailed contents page and a glossary and index; after the first read to find out what happens to Jake, the book could then be used for a lot of research of all kinds. One of the book's great strengths, as we hope to go on to illustrate, is that it inspires and enthuses the reader to want to find out more about a wide range of topics.

Controversial issues in the text

Richard Platt, the author, does not shrink from tackling some controversial topics. The ship that Jake initially sets sail on is dealing in contraband goods – the crew are smugglers. Jake's home is Charleston, on the east coast of America, and at the time, this area was part of the British American colonies. The sailors' point of view is 'Why should we Americans pay taxes to an English king?' (p. 13). There are notes at the back of the book that attempt to take some of the issues further, although inevitably they are very brief. Nothing is said about the rights or wrongs of colonialism, although we are given the information that some colonists were killed by Native Americans on whose land the colonists had built their farms.

Later, Jake's ship is seized by pirates, and so the author must help his young readers to understand something of the moral issues surrounding piracy. These are much more complex than many of them will have been led to believe. The pirates have taken to the life because they are discontented with the way the English rule their American colonies. Both sides of the argument, for and against piracy, are explained in the text itself and in the notes (though we suspect most young readers will find the latter rather condensed and difficult to follow). Children reading the book, therefore, are placed by the author in a position to judge for themselves about piracy to some extent. One would expect them to see the issues through the American Jake's eyes but he is cleverly shown weighing up all sides of the argument and so we are forced to do so too: ' "For myself," he says, "I could not decide who was right or wrong" ' (p. 23).

Difficult issues are not shirked and include death (in battle and by hanging), amputation (without anaesthetic of course), sex and violence. Readers are not spared horrific details, in both the text and illustrations, which show that rough justice was dealt out by both the smugglers and the pirates – but then this was a violent time and we are told that many of the sailors on Jake's ship felt that they had been just as badly off before the pirate takeover. Several floggings are described, for example, that were instigated by the ship's captain: 'The poor seaman was forced to whip until his friend's blood sprayed upon the deck. I turned away, but saw those behind me flinch each time the whip came down' (p. 17).

The pirates on the other hand are shown to be very fair in their way of organising themselves, electing their own leader and scrupulously following rules or 'articles' that have been democratically drawn up. One of these is that anyone caught 'meddling' with a prudent woman, without her consent, 'shall suffer death'.

Characters

Jake himself is a complete novice about life at sea. As this is his journal, written in the first person, we learn as he learns. One way of learning is to ask lots of questions. The author provides him with a variety of sources of information:

- Jake's uncle is there to explain and comment from an adult perspective. For example, he advises Jake not to ask too many questions about where the ship is going, or about its cargo.

- Jake is also provided with a different kind of informant, one of his own age. This is Abraham, the cook's boy, who can, for example, tell Jake about the delights of ship's biscuits. They're full of maggots, so you either eat them in the dark, or, if you can't wait, you tap them hard and most of the maggots fall out. Abraham is used by the writer to overcome another problem associated with first person writing. There are some facts that the 'I' character – the 'writer' – is ignorant about. Jake doesn't know where the ship is going, so Abraham steals a chart from the captain's cabin for him to look at. The author then has to account for why Abraham should be so helpful. The answer is that he wants Jake to teach him to read and write. The value and usefulness of literacy are well argued throughout the whole text.

Text layout and illustrations

We've already said that this is a book pretending to be something it isn't. One reason why we say this is that it is vividly illustrated. Jake could supposedly be a good water colourist as well as an expert storyteller but he never comments on this or on where he might have got the materials. An interesting feature of the text structure is that we are several times given a vivid verbal account of an incident and only afterwards shown a double-page picture of it. This happens when the pirates take over the ship, for example, and when they attack a Spanish crew and steal their treasure. It's sometimes said that children's books these days are over-illustrated, so that children become dependent on the artist's imagination, rather than their own. Here we readers have done the imaginative work, as it were, and then we turn over and find the artist's version, which could lead to some interesting discussion about interpretation.

Sometimes, illustrations seem to invite child readers to do the further research we mentioned. We are told, for example (p. 13), that Jake was ordered to work as a servant for Adam, the carpenter, who 'has taught me the names of all his tools so that I can hand them to him when he needs them'. We see Jake gazing in a puzzled way at the tools laid out on the deck, inviting us, the readers, to find out which is which.

Sentence structure

The writer gives the syntax an eighteenth-century flavour, without allowing it to become too intrusive. Examples include:

- 'It is the third year of the reign of our good king George and the tenth of my life' (p. 5).
- 'I knew not my mother for she died when I was yet a baby' (p. 5).
- 'My aunts both hugged me and dabbed my eyes with their aprons (though they would have better dabbed their own, which needed it more)' (p. 7).

As this is a journal, one might have expected more incomplete sentences – with the subject missing. In fact this only happens once:

- 'Thursday, 11th. Saw a man flogged' (p. 17).

Because the ellipsis is used at such a dramatic moment, it helps to heighten the drama of the narrative.

Words

Archaisms

There are some archaisms but they are used sparingly and don't obscure the meaning for present-day young readers. Examples include:

- 'This was my only schooling' (p. 5).
- 'Strange gifts and wondrous yarns [i.e. stories]' (p. 5).
- 'This morn . . . I was sorely disappointed' (p. 7).

Technical terms

The author exploits Jake's ignorance to explain various technical terms to us the readers. As well as clearly labelled diagrams, included as Jake tries to find his way around the ship, there are verbal explanations:

- 'They did this [i.e. loading cargo] with the aid of one of the ship's yards [these being the stout timbers crossing the mast, from which the sails hang]' (p. 10).

As Jake comes to terms with aspects of life on board ship, so the young reader can be reminded of what life was like in the eighteenth century – no electricity, for example:

- 'Here I must end, for daylight fades. Candles are permitted only inside a horn lantern, which protects the ship against fire' (p. 10).

Again, just enough is said to intrigue the readers and hopefully stimulate them to find out more. There is a combined glossary and index that explains unusual words the pirates would have used, or refers readers to explanations in the text.

People Who Made History: Native Americans, Jason Hook, illustrated by Richard Hook, Hodder Wayland, 2000

What kind of text is this?

Of all the books in this chapter on non-fiction texts, this one is most typical of the kind of information text that children will find themselves using in many areas of the curriculum, but especially in history and geography. It is a report text, using Wray and Lewis's (1997) classifications. It's the kind of text that can be abused by children in their project work because they have sometimes been tempted to copy chunks from books like this, straight into their own writing folders. This misdemeanour is immediately apparent to their teachers because of the 'textbook' style of the writing (p. 15):

> Like King Philip, Tecumseh saw the need for Indian nations to unite in defence of their land. In his youth, he had seen his father and two brothers killed by the settlers, now known as Americans, and had watched his chiefs sign away much of the Shawnee lands.

We don't intend any criticism of the book in labelling it thus. It's full of interesting material and reasonably accessible to Key Stage 2 readers, though not many children would read it from end to end. It would be a good text to use to discuss with children how to access information and make notes.

Accessing the information

The author has provided plenty of support in the form of a clear contents page, plenty of headings and subheadings, information in boxes, a timeline and an index and a glossary. There's an interesting mixture of portraits and photographs so that teachers can explore what each of these can contribute to our knowledge of the topic. Even children who are just 'flicking through' the book are helped by a list of the names of all the people who've been written about down the right-hand edge. The name of the particular person dealt with on each page is printed in bold. Readers are encouraged to explore the topic further for themselves; there are books to read and two websites are suggested.

Developing critical reading skills

One reason why we chose to discuss this text was because of its links with the previous one. *Pirate Diary* presents children with a picture of American settlers that they may well be familiar with from books and movies. Jake sets off on his travels from a white-painted clapboard house that could have come straight from *Anne of Green Gables*. Native Americans are given the briefest of mentions, in the notes. We thought it would be interesting therefore to place that book side by side with one that sets out to explore the Native Americans' history – preferably from their perspective. We think this text achieves that reasonably well.

It is very important for children to be encouraged to read critically. Becoming a critical reader means asking searching questions at the text level, such as:

- Why have I been given these particular facts?
- Might there have been significant facts that were omitted?
- Can I believe the facts I've been given?
- Why has this picture been used?
- Why has the page been laid out in this way?

At the sentence and word levels, readers need continually to ask themselves:

- Why this particular language?
- Could other words have been used instead?
- What would the effect have been then?
- Why this juxtaposition of ideas in this sentence?

It's very clear from the contents page that Jason Hook has chosen to organise his selection of facts around famous names from Native American history. Apart from an introduction and a conclusion, these names form the titles of all the sections. Readers are thus shown the 'bravest and best' with a list of impressive achievements clearly documented. Here are a few examples:

- Tecumseh was said to be 'a magnificent speaker'.
- Sequoyah was a talented painter, a genius who invented a Cherokee alphabet.
- Sacajawea was able to take her baby on expeditions because of the excellent design of Indian baby carriers.

The book uses portraits and photographs that enhance the dignity of the subjects. Each person's picture features prominently on his or her pages. Each section contains a short 'curriculum vitae' of the person concerned, ending with something said about them, usually by a white settler. Again, each of these quotations has obviously been carefully chosen to enhance their reputation. So Captain J.G. Bourke said of Crazy Horse: 'Justly regarded as the boldest, bravest and most skilful warrior in the whole Sioux nation' (p. 36). General Miles is quoted as saying, 'Think we shall make short work of it' (p. 28), before Chief Joseph outwitted his troops for 108 days.

Of course, we probably all feel that it is high time that the Native Americans were given more credit for their sophisticated culture and their incredible bravery and endurance. But the fact that the portrayal of them here is one that most of us would be happy to see does not diminish the importance of reminding young readers of the points we made above. To summarise, any account is a selection of all that could have been said. Just as in analysing a media text, children should be reminded that the camera has been pointed in one direction and therefore a particular impression has been given and other features of the scene have had to be left unrecorded.

Word choice

If an extract from this text were to be used for class discussion (because, as we have said, this is not a book for reading from beginning to end), it might be interesting to choose the section dealing with Crazy Horse. He was one of the chiefs who met with General Custer's 7th Cavalry at Little Bighorn. Plenty of accounts of this episode can be found to compare with this one. In this book we read (p. 36):

On 25 June 1876, George Armstrong Custer's 7th Cavalry attacked a huge Indian camp at Little Bighorn. Crazy Horse's warriors fought back furiously, killing every one of Custer's 215 men. One Indian warrior said of Crazy Horse: 'All the soldiers were shooting at him, but he was never hit.'

We are given the idea of intense bravery on the part of the Indians, defending themselves against Custer's attack, with the Indian leader having an almost mystical ability to escape death. Yet other accounts you can find speak of '[white] men dying to try to save their doomed comrades from the ravening hordes [of Indians]' and 'too many howling red attackers to resist'. You can find writers who describe how the Indians were 'extracting their blood-thirsty revenge' on the white men. The only hint of this treatment of the episode in Jason Hook's text is on page 37 where we can see a facsimile of a small piece of the *Chicago Daily* for 6 July 1876. Above a map of the area a headline reads 'Scene of the Massacre' and of course it is thus that the event has often been described.

Summary

In this chapter we have discussed applying text-, sentence- and word-level knowledge to:

- *Splish, Splash, Splosh! A Book about Water* by Mick Manning and Brita Granstrom;

- *Spider Watching* by Vivian French;

- *Pirate Diary. The Journal of Jake Carpenter* by Richard Platt and Chris Riddell;

- *People Who Made History: Native Americans* by Jason Hook and Richard Hook.

11

Applying text-, sentence- and word-level knowledge to non-book and electronic texts

The term 'non-book' covers a multitude of publications, often referred to as 'media texts', from comics and newspapers to promotional and advertising leaflets and electronic texts. Electronic texts are those that can be transmitted through an electronic medium, such as a computer, and therefore cover websites, CD-ROMs and the like.

This chapter will focus on a sample of non-book and electronic texts and will consider the skills and knowledge needed to make sense of them. The text types covered will include:

- comic strips;
- promotional leaflets;
- CD-ROMs;
- websites (social networking websites will be considered in Chapter 12).

Where possible, we will compare the features of each text type to those of a conventional book text.

The relevance of media texts

From an early age children are aware of the visual impact of signs, symbols and logos. One little boy, at the age of two and a half, would shout, 'Ah, someone cares!' each time he passed a Boots lorry on the motorway. What he was shouting was, of course, the Boots TV advertising slogan at the time, thus suggesting his ability to both recognise and link a logo with a product, despite a lack of understanding of meaning. There is no doubt that our world is one of visual stimuli and developing communications and technologies. Children need to be made aware of how to handle texts that belong to this new age and understand how language is being adapted to different situations. After all, 'what was basic literacy two decades ago is not compatible with current needs' (Craggs 1992: 3). As long ago as 1999, the National Curriculum recognised the fact that children need to be prepared to live in a rapidly changing world and part of this preparation is the ability to read and interpret a range of media texts. Making sense of so-called non-literary texts requires enhanced reading skills as the reader must learn a set of codes or conventions and in many cases must deconstruct the text (take it apart and consider why the author created it in a particular way) to interpret its meaning. In addition, such texts 'must be looked at in the context of the choice of modes made, the modes which appear with the writing' (Kress 2003: 11). The most common mode to appear with writing is the image, but music, colour and moving image are also possible. Therefore, it is important for us, as adults, to be aware of changing language conventions.

Comics and graphic books

Comics are probably the most familiar non-electronic media text type available to children. Our memories are of piles of comics being placed on the desk by the teacher during wet playtime. This act was representative of the attitude towards comics that prevailed then and, to a certain extent, persists today: that they are a bit of fun, not a proper read with any educational value. The fact is, however, that they are very cleverly put together and follow their own generic structure and format. It is necessary to know how to read a comic in order to fully understand its content. This knowledge can then be applied to the increasingly popular genre of children's books, the graphic novel.

The structure of a comic strip

A comic strip is split into boxes or 'frames'. Within each frame the story is developed in three ways:

- *Graphics.* The drawings are visually descriptive, showing actions and scenes. They are crucial in providing information about characters and settings, as written words are limited in number.

- *Speech and thought bubbles.* The story is told mainly through dialogue in the form of speech and thought bubbles. There are a range of bubble types to indicate whispering, shouting, thinking and so on (Figure 11.1).

- *Story narration and time-lapse boxes.* The frame is often split to show a small box at the top that will outline the story, provide a link or detail a setting.

Therefore, the ability to enjoy a comic strip is dependent primarily upon the reader being able to read and interpret a 'complicated system of signs and symbols' (Craggs 1992: 23).

FIGURE 11.1 A range of bubble types, from Byrne (2003).

Comic strip language

Generally there is a tendency towards more colloquial informal language, mainly because the largest proportion of the written language is in the form of dialogue. The titles of each story or strip can be likened to a newspaper article in that they often involve puns, alliteration or rhyme. By studying a specific comic strip in more detail, it is possible to identify the features of structure and style. In the more traditional comics the language is often dated.

The Beano, No. 3216, 6 March 2004

What kind of text is this?

This is a classic comic generally considered to be aimed primarily at boys (it is interesting to compare the content and style with that of a 'girl's' comic such as *Girl Talk*). The main characters are children who tend to be anarchic, showing little respect for adults or authority. At text level it is important to discuss actions, attitudes and behaviours, mainly because a typical comic strip will challenge our own cultural and moral values by condoning what the government would deem antisocial behaviours!

Dennis the Menace and Minnie the Minx are probably two of the best-known comic characters and both feature in this publication. We will now look at the 'Minnie the Minx' feature from the issue detailed above.

The title

The definition of the word 'minx' is 'sly girl' or 'hussy' (Fowler *et al.* 1996). This immediately conjures up an image of her character and, combined with the use of both alliteration (the repeated 'm' sound at the beginning of each noun) and assonance (the repeated short vowel sound /i/), does indeed make the title memorable!

The plot and characters

In brief, Minnie is taken to 'Crumbly Castle', the alliterative 'crumbly' suggesting its state of repair. The first frame makes it clear that she does not want to be there. The plot is developed by Minnie stealing sausages from an out-of-place burger bar and dropping a cannonball on the foot of a museum official, in keeping with character expectations. The final frames show Minnie being caught and humiliated in the stocks, her anger at which is made clear through facial expression and dialogue, as she calls her punishers 'dirty rotters'.

As with any narrative text, actions and dialogue are key to building up character descriptions. Comics have the added advantage of a picture description. Minnie can be seen wearing a striped jumper, similar to that of her fellow *Beano* star, Dennis the Menace. This is an example of graphic intertextuality, and the reader's expectations of both characters will be the same.

In this feature, the yellow 'time-lapse' boxes at the top of selected frames contain single connectives such as 'then', 'shortly' and 'next' to add cohesion to the text by ordering it chronologically.

Text construction and choice of words

Words are chosen carefully for maximum impact and, because the emphasis is on dialogue, the written syntax is the same as that of spontaneous speech. In the first frame the more formal dialogue of Minnie's father, who says, 'Going around this old castle will be jolly interesting, Minnie', is contrasted sharply with Minnie's more colloquial response, 'Hmph! Borin' ol' place is deserted'. The final letters of 'boring' and 'old' are replaced with apostrophes and are examples of elision. The author has chosen to miss the final sounds from words to suggest that a young person is speaking and in this case the method works. The reader is immediately aware that these words are spoken by a younger person, without having to look at the supporting graphics for confirmation. The adult characters all tend to speak in complete sentences with a more formal tone.

Despite there being a clear difference between the adult and child language within the text, in general the language is very dated. Examples are 'dirty rotters' and the use of the word 'hooter' to mean 'nose'. Interestingly, this use of dated language does not appear to affect children's enjoyment of the comic. In fact, Julie's son found it very amusing to refer to everyone's nose as their 'hooter' for weeks after reading this strip! The text also contains a number of invented words, such as 'squoylch', which could be derived from 'squash' and 'squelch' and so is immediately identifiable. Others need to be read in conjunction with the graphics to give a clearer meaning, for example 'GNNOINK!' The capitalisation and punctuation show that it is a shouted exclamation, but seeing the picture of the character having his nose squashed immediately causes the reader to focus on the 'oink' part of the word, which has connotations with pigs and snouts.

Sounds also play a huge part in this comic strip, from the noises characters are making to the noise made by instruments from the torture chamber and sausages 'sizzling'. This, like most of the words used in the feature to suggest noise, is an example of onomatopoeia, but it is also a particularly interesting example of *suggested* alliteration. The phrase 'sausages sizzling on a sword' is created through graphics, and the only written word is 'sizzle' (see Figure 11.2).

Graphics

Using Figure 11.2 as an example, we can see a wide range of graphic devices being used in both the pictures and the typeset. There is a standard speech bubble to identify dialogue but the most interesting features are the three different ways that noise is represented:

- jagged lines;

FIGURE 11.2 Minnie the Minx from *The Beano*, No. 3216, 6 March 2004.

- bold type;
- bubble type and capitalisation.

In each case the text is followed by an exclamation mark, which suggests a display of emotion in each case: 'OY!' suggests anger, 'ZOOM!' determination and 'SIZZLE!' has humorous effect. The word 'ZOOM' also suggests movement. This is apparent by its increasing size from left to right.

The knowledge and understanding of visual literacy needed to read and appreciate *The Beano* can be applied to all comic features including graphic books and some websites that have adopted this style.

Graphic books

Graphic books are picture books that use the same layout and language conventions as comics. They are available in a range of genres.

Ug, Boy Genius of the Stone Age by Raymond Briggs, Jonathan Cape, 2001

What kind of text is this?

This is an excellent example of a modern graphic book that can be appreciated by adults and children alike. The blurb on the cover sheet describes the book as 'thought-provoking' and at text level it raises a number of issues for discussion, including hardship, determination, failure, being controlled and bereavement.

The plot

The book tells the story of a Stone Age boy, Ug, who lives with his parents Dug (dad) and Dugs (mum) in a stone house, wears stone trousers and sleeps on a stone bed with a stone cover. His one desire is to have soft trousers, and in his quest to obtain them he has a whole host of ideas to improve life, but, sadly, he isn't taken seriously, especially by his mother. At the end Ug is an adult, his parents are dead and, although he is obviously sad, wishing he wasn't living in the Stone Age, he remains convinced that things **'MUST'** get better. The author uses capitalisation and bold type to emphasise the positive.

There are four main levels to this text and all must be explored and understood to appreciate the work in its entirety. They are:

- The storyline (as outlined above). Interestingly it is also historically informative, so much so that some suppliers categorise the work as non-fiction.
- Humour, often as a result of Mum's despair at her son and the comments this emotion provokes: 'Mark my words – he'll go mad, that boy. He'll end up painting animals on the walls.' The reader needs to have some knowledge of future developments to appreciate the humour of this.
- Anachronisms. The text, like a non-fiction text, has a series of footnotes, in this case anachronisms because they explain why many of the words used in the

dialogue represent items or features not from the Stone Age period, for example nails.

- Graphics. The pictures are of a high quality and are subtly detailed, even showing Ug ageing by the length of his stone trousers. Therefore, the graphics play an important role in the cohesion of this text.

Word choices and sentence structure

The characters' names, Ug, Dug and Dugs and Ag (Ug's friend), suggest the grunts and limited speech associated with the Stone Age. But this is the only gesture to primitive language, hence the anachronisms. The anachronisms (a challenging piece of vocabulary itself!) are more formally structured than the dialogue and use full sentences. They can be likened to encyclopaedia references; for example 'Iron: Iron did not exist in the Stone Age. Iron was invented in the Iron Age which came much later, 4000BC to 2000BC and so gave its name to the Iron Age.' However, some of the vocabulary within the anachronisms is colloquial: 'Wood . . . they did not realise the trees were chock-a-block with it.' There are more examples of slang in the dialogue. On page 7, Dad Dug introduces the concept of 'youth culture' and talks about children having their own 'lingo'.

The whole text is written in upper case, rather like a young child's first attempts at writing, and this gives it a more primitive feel. Mum shouts a lot and much of her conversation is in large bold type with exclamation marks to show her frustration. The piece is descriptive, with a range of adjectives, as in 'Trousers out of a baby mammoth? They'd be all soft and floppy', and similes: 'You'll have to be tough THEN! Tough as old boots.'

On the whole this text succeeds in making the reader empathise with a little boy, desperate to make himself heard. We understand; we've all been there!

Tourist information promotional leaflets

Promotional leaflets provide a most colourful and accessible route into persuasive writing. Tourist attraction leaflets are readily available and offer opportunities to compare layout and language. All such leaflets can be broken down into three main parts: cover, centre and back page. These parts all serve particular purposes. The cover is designed to attract the attention of the target audience and persuade them to pick up the leaflet. An eye-catching picture and persuasive text work together to achieve this. The centre of the leaflet will give some information about the place itself, often in the form of a labelled map, bullet points or headings. The back of the leaflet will contain essential information: opening times, cost, facilities, location and so on.

The Blue Planet Aquarium (www.blueplanetaquarium.com)

What kind of text is this?

This is a persuasive text promoting the Blue Planet Aquarium, a large indoor attraction in the north-west of England. It is set out in typical leaflet fashion, as previously described, but there are some noticeable omissions, which will be considered later.

The leaflet itself is of a standard length and width with four folds. Size is important for tourist information leaflets as they are generally distributed to hotels where they are displayed in a wire 'pouch' and they have to be made to fit! The cover has an eye-catching and colourful picture of a range of sea creatures, the most impressive of which is a huge and intimidating shark. In sharp contrast to the shark are two clownfish, a seahorse and a blue starfish. Inclusion of the clownfish provides an intertextual link to the Disney film 'Finding Nemo'. The picture suggests that:

- the exhibits live in harmony together;
- the exhibits are very impressive and out of the ordinary.

Both the picture and the written words play on the fear aspect, suggesting that visitors will come close to danger in the form of sharks (the picture shows a shark presiding over all of the other creatures) and poisonous animals. There is a new attraction for 2010 called 'Venom' and the written text presents the potential visitor with the ultimate challenge '*Face Your Fears VENOM!*' The font style is gothic and its colour is white set within a red splat, suggesting that the words are etched in a pool of blood. This attraction is obviously not for the faint-hearted, although a picture of a screaming boy's head inside a glass dome surrounded by various tarantula spiders suggests that the danger will be encountered in a safe environment. The intended audience is made clear as we open the leaflet. Inside there are a number of pictures suggesting that there is something for all the family: a father is pictured pointing at a ray with his smiling daughter, a mother is holding her son as he meets 'Charlie the Clownfish', an older boy is handling a starfish and there are a boy and a girl blowing out nine candles on a birthday cake.

In its effort to persuade you to visit, the leaflet has a number of interesting features:

- The experience will be not only entertaining but also educational because of the staff's professional expertise. Visitors can 'Enjoy shows and talks on a selection of our 50 exhibits or watch the team feed our 700 fish in our Caribbean Reef Exhibit'.
- The map on the back of the leaflet shows the Blue Planet Aquarium and the major motorway and trunk roads, which end in arrow heads pointing in the direction of a major city or region: Preston, Manchester, Birmingham, North Wales, and so on. This suggests to the reader that the venue is easily accessible from the Midlands as well as the north-west, and therefore that distance is no barrier.
- It is probably expensive and subject to change as no price is quoted.
- The cost is irrelevant as there is so much to see.
- Exhibits must change regularly as annual pass holders are encouraged to '*Visit Again and Again and Again!*'

As noted, what is not included is the cost of admission for a single visit. Annual passes are advertised but no price is quoted for these either. Across the bottom of the unfolded leaflet, and at the bottom of the 'How To Find Us' section, is the sentence 'Buy tickets online at: www.blueplanetaquarium.com.' This approach is, in its own way, persuasive and suggests that you should buy your ticket from your home, at any time, day or night, to avoid disappointment.

Throughout the text, information is presented under very bold headings, and the use of photographs not only makes it visually stimulating but also reinforces the written information provided.

Text construction and choice of words

There are numerous examples of verbs in their imperative (command) form; for example '*Hop* over to our poisonous frog zone' and '*View* our 3.8 million litre Caribbean Reef Exhibit home to Southern Stingrays and Europe's largest collection of sharks'. This particular sentence offers the opportunity to examine superlative adjectives such as 'largest'. Another example in the text is 'deadliest': 'Come face to face with the planet's deadliest creatures'.

There are examples of persuasive phrases, such as 'and much, much more', and sentences, such as 'Enjoy an unforgettable undersea themed party including a tour of the aquarium, free face painting and a selection of party food'. A number of exclamations such as 'there's a world of pain to explore!' not only create a wow factor but also almost dare you to visit. There is also use of a double exclamation mark 'Venom – Face your Fears!!' for additional effect. Capitalisation of the letter 'F' in 'Face' and 'Fears' suggests an enormous challenge.

The tone of the text is informal with much use of the first person plural 'we'; for example 'we also have a breathtaking array of over 50 exhibits for the whole family!' This suggests a group of people inviting the visitor into the attraction and as such it suggests a personal and informal experience. In addition there are a number of examples of elision (see p. 55): 'there is' is shortened to 'there's'. This demonstrates the use of an apostrophe to mark a contraction, which is expected in informal writing and speech.

There are a number of examples of alliteration including 'Venom – Face your Fears'; as with a newspaper headline it grabs attention. Another example is 'Tarantula Tower – Step inside our incredible transparent tower and be surrounded by tarantulas'. The word 'incredible' is very persuasive, suggesting that it should not be missed. Other examples of persuasive vocabulary in the leaflet are 'awesome' and 'breathtaking' and 'impressive'. The exhibits are described using interesting adjectives. Seahorses are *magical* creatures, and there are *sinister* scorpions, *toxic* reptiles, *deadly* stonefish, *adorable* otters and *friendly* rays. Undoubtedly the descriptions are carefully crafted, none more so than that of the rays, which are 'friendly' allowing you to 'stroke and interact' with them in the 'Hands on Experience' section, yet are described as 'stingrays' in the 'Sharks' section. An intentional contradiction we think!

It is interesting to compare the persuasive language in such leaflets with posters and with print and television advertisements.

CD-ROMs

CD-ROMs fall into two main categories:

- reference;
- interactive.

Until recently a CD-ROM was used by one or two children at a time to research a given topic or to complete an activity in the form of a game. This can be a problem, as it is difficult to ensure that the children stay focused on a particular objective. Advances in presentational technologies, such as the interactive whiteboard, have meant that CD-ROMs can now be viewed by the whole class, as can websites of course. This also allows the teacher to emphasise an objective and keep the class focused. Recent research has found that 'The teacher's use of ICT as a presentational aid helps to focus pupils' attention during whole class teaching' (University of Newcastle 1999: 4). Therefore, a clear understanding about how language is used and how features are organised can be considered essential for both successful teaching and successful learning.

Reference CD-ROMs

Widely used encyclopaedias, such as *Encarta*, are probably the best known in this category. Essentially the information is ordered and presented in the same way as in a book. The text is read from left to right, the information is ordered alphabetically and the user can search an index to find a chosen subject. The only real difference is that there are no pages to turn!

Interactive CD-ROMs

These offer the user an opportunity to carry out an activity such as a simple game to support their learning.

The New Way Things Work, Dorling Kindersley (Key Stage 2)

What kind of CD-ROM is this?

This is a reference CD-ROM with limited but effective interactive sequences. It is science based and offers information about:

- scientific principles, in the form of explanations;
- the history of science, in the form of a timeline;
- inventors, in the form of short biographies.

This gives the user an opportunity to explore the generic features of various non-fiction text types.

Presentation of information

The way in which the main menu page is presented lacks clarity, although there is a helpful static menu running down the left-hand side of the screen. This consists of an icon and a single-word description of what it does: for example two cogs represent 'machines'. In addition to the static menu, the page is dominated by a picture in which many of the menu icons appear, allowing the user to navigate the program from a main picture rather than from the menu. Therefore, as with other media texts, the user has to become familiar with a range of symbols to use the product effectively. This can cause problems in that it is tempting to explore the options in the picture rather than to remain focused on the learning objective.

As with a conventional text, each section has an alphabetical index, for example 'An A–Z of Machines'. One area, the 'Digital Domain', is focused on new technologies and each subject has an icon to support its written form in this area's index, which is set out like the page on a PC. The user moves the cursor to a chosen subject such as 'DVD-ROM', and an explanation appears, complete with diagram.

The diagram

The diagrams are clearly labelled and the user can bring the diagram to life by moving the cursor to 'Make it work' and left clicking the mouse. The moving diagram offers a spoken dialogue that adds to the original written explanation. There are also useful and captivating sound effects, especially for explanations about flight and jet engines!

Vocabulary

Some words in the text and some diagram labels appear in red type. They are usually examples of difficult, scientific vocabulary for which a definition may be useful, and the user can click on these red, highlighted words to obtain a further explanation or definition. However, this can cause problems with focus as the user can move off at a tangent.

Pingu, BBC Multimedia (Key Stage 1)

What kind of CD-ROM is this?

This is very much an interactive CD-ROM offering a range of activities in the forms of games, puzzles and screen savers, all of which support literacy, numeracy and music in the curriculum. From a language perspective, the activities are based at word level only. They are representative of similar products used frequently in schools to support spelling.

Presentation of information

The information is clearly presented throughout. The main menu page displays Pingu standing below the three menu choices of puzzles, games and screen savers. Each is supported by an icon and is spoken to the user as the pointer or cursor is passed over it, allowing the non-reader to make use of the programs. There is also a selection of three colour-coded buttons at the bottom of the page:

- volume (pink);
- quit (red) – this changes to 'stop' during the activities;
- help (yellow);
- dance (green).

The red and yellow buttons remain throughout. When the user selects a preference, a sub-menu will appear showing the options in a particular category (five puzzles in the puzzle menu).

Letter puzzle (literacy)

There are two levels of puzzle. Level 1 deals with the initial phoneme (sound) in simple CVC (consonant, vowel, consonant) words such as 'dog'. The 'og' is given and a picture of a dog is shown. The user then chooses the initial letter from a selection. The letters are sounded out as the pointer is passed over them. In Level 2 the word is 'spelt out' with the correct number of dashes. Again there is a picture clue and a selection of letters that have to be selected in the right order. With the word 'apple', for example, the selection of letters is 'a', 'k', 'p', 'l', 'y', 'l', 'e'. Therefore a letter may be used more than once, so the user must be familiar with simple spelling patterns to avoid frustration.

Graphics

The pictures are simple, clear and colourful. The graphics are consistent throughout the programs, adding a degree of familiarity and continuity.

CD-ROMs are undoubtedly an engaging way of supporting learning and children are clearly motivated by them. Selecting an appropriate CD-ROM is like selecting a book in that it is essential to ensure that layout, content and language are appropriate.

Websites

Most of us use the internet regularly and have come to understand its importance for finding information, buying and selling goods and communicating with friends. There are both similarities and differences between retrieving and reading information from a website and obtaining the information from a conventional non-fiction text. First we would like to consider aspects of grammar in relation to web pages before looking at some of the barriers to information retrieval.

The web address

We will concentrate on the BBC TV website throughout this section as it is popular not only with schools because of its educational value but also with adults and children in the home. It is important to consider the syntax of the address itself and how punctuation terminology has evolved through usage. This presents teachers with a great opportunity to encourage children to think about and discuss punctuation.

- www.bbc.co.uk

As users of the internet, we know that 'www' is an acronym for 'World Wide Web' and that it is followed by a full stop, which is referred to as a 'dot'. The dot is not recognised as a full stop in this situation and is an example of the evolution of punctuation. The 'forward slash' is another example, as inexperienced web users will often refer to it in a more traditional way, as an oblique.

- www.bbc.co.uk/cbbc

The letters in the BBC's web address are lower case, despite the fact that capital letters are usually seen at the beginning of each word. This is typical of all web addresses: letters (including those at the beginning of proper nouns) are generally written in lower case.

The homepage

The majority of websites will have a homepage, which works in a similar way to the contents page and introduction of a non-fiction reference book. It will provide information about the site (introduction) and links to other parts of the site (contents). The main differences between a website and a conventional text are:

- layout;
- inclusion of advertising material (limited on non-commercial sites);
- moving and static images.

The BBC's homepage, May 2010

Web pages tend to be very busy with lots going on and the BBC's homepage is no exception, although it has changed considerably in recent years! Learning to navigate a website and discard irrelevant information in order to find a relevant page is a crucial part of the reading process that a child will not generally encounter with a more conventional print text.

Layout

At the top of the page is a navigation bar providing access to the most popular sites across the BBC and a search facility (see Figure 11.3). Most homepages will have this facility, allowing the user to type in a keyword and search the site. The BBC search facility also includes a 'more' drop-down menu if you do not want to type in a keyword. The drop-down menu includes an A–Z listing. These facilities allow the user to discard the other information on the page. The search facility can be sited anywhere on the page but is usually found at the top right-hand corner. Note that it is important to encourage children to locate the search facility and use it, as it maintains a focus and stops time being wasted. Like us, you have probably spent hours searching websites and being distracted because something looked interesting! Keep this in mind.

Advertising is limited to forthcoming TV programmes and BBC products or features and can be found below the navigation bar in a horizontally aligned module. The main advertisement is for the upcoming Eurovision Song Contest and is in the form of a captivating photographic image with a simple statement, 'How to write the winning Eurovision lyric'. This is accompanied by links to supporting web pages

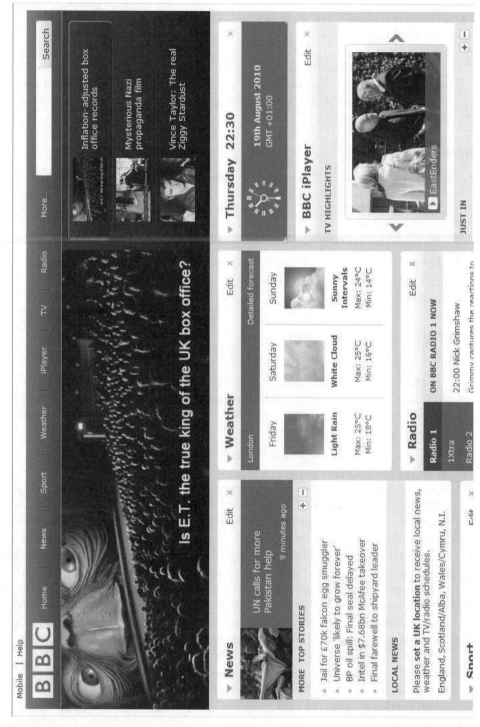

FIGURE 11.3 An example of the BBC homepage – August 2010.

such as 'Winning Words', 'Learn the Lingo' (both good examples of alliteration). The remaining modules are aligned vertically in columns across the page and consist of News, Weather, TV etc. The BBC uses a variety of symbols. There are universally accepted symbols to show weather conditions, such as a yellow sun on a blue background representing 'sunny', and others that would, without explanation, be known only to users of specific media, for example 'cbbc' will be most recognizable to children, parents/carers and teachers (see Figure 11.4).

This set of symbols, and others like them, are known as 'icons'. This is an example of how language and word usage evolves (the word icon having been traditionally associated with sacred images, not computer symbols). Of course, the extensive use of symbols across all areas of information technology is another example of the importance of understanding visual literacy. The symbols on this homepage are static, that is, they remain in position.

Text construction and choice of words

Like a newspaper, the information is given in a series of headlines:

- Gun fights flare in Pakistan city

The sentence begins with a capital letter but does not end with a full stop, which is a feature of any headline. Another common feature of a headline is the use of alliteration, in this case the repeated 'f' at the start of 'fights' and 'flare'. You can almost hear a newspaper seller shouting this headline as you read it. It is written in the present tense, suggesting breaking news, and this has the effect of making the reader want to read on and find out more. The sentence structure is informal giving rise to an ellipsis in that the use of the indefinite article 'a' before 'Pakistan' would complete the sentence.

Children's BBC (www.bbc.co.uk/cbbc)

What kind of text is this?

The homepage layout for Children's BBC contains less written text and more images in the form of pictures, photographs and icons. It is clear that the BBC have designed their web pages in a consistent modular format. At the top of the page is a noises/images on/off option allowing the user to opt for an additional mode of interactivity through the use of sound and moving image. The sounds on the homepage relate

FIGURE 11.4 Two of the symbols used on the BBC website.

to a fantastical wildlife scene and are reminiscent of rainforest noises. Across the top of the page is an option for an A–Z 'alphabetic' listing with an alternative visual representation. In the visual representation, familiar programme titles and their logos appear in the form of a bar. This scrolls over to reveal more programmes when the user clicks on the 'pull' bar. This facility has been created to look like an old-fashioned, one-armed bandit. This means that it remains permanently displayed even if the reader scrolls down the page. The CBBC logo, displayed at the top of the right-hand vertical 'i-player' module, spins as the curser moves across it, both amusing the reader and confirming that the desired page has been accessed. However, it is an example of web page material that can otherwise be ignored.

Text construction and choice of words

At the bottom of the web page is a 'Newsround' repeating headlines section. The user can view the headlines as they move across the page on a continuous link and click on a 'Read more' button if they want further details. It is interesting that the serious 'world news' roundup concludes with a lighter 'feel-good' headline, typical of the structure of TV news. For example, 'Oil spill is worst in US history' is followed by 'Kitten survives washer spin cycle'. As with the news on the main BBC homepage, the information is in newspaper headline format. In the two 'headlines' we see an example of an abbreviation, as United States becomes 'US', and an example of alliteration, in the form of the repetition of the letter 's' in 'survives' and 'spin'. The sentence structures are informal with an ellipsis in the headline 'Oil spill is worst in US history' as the definite article 'the' before 'worst' is omitted. In the headline ' Kitten survives washer spin cycle' we assume that 'washer' is a washing machine. Selection of the less formal word 'washer' makes the headline short and punchy.

When accessing web pages it must be remembered that no two are exactly the same. However, many of the features discussed in relation to the BBC can be found throughout the World Wide Web. It is also important to bear in mind that there is a lot of information out there in various forms such as explanations, discussions, arguments and reports. The main function of any web page is to provide information and, as with any other information text, the reader has to evaluate the information by:

- reading critically;
- establishing the credibility of the source;
- considering the reliability of the information provided (see Chapter 10, p. 128).

This chapter has provided an insight into the language conventions of some non-book and electronic texts. Of course, it represents only a small sample of such text types. You may wish to consider applying this knowledge to e-mail, newspapers and advertising posters and their TV and radio equivalents. In all cases such media texts provide the teacher with opportunities to explore language from a perspective that children find stimulating and motivating. It can be a truly shared experience as it brings teacher and pupils together – the children view it as their teacher entering their world.

Being familiar with a range of media texts is undoubtedly an essential ingredient of language education. Why essential? The answer can be summed up in a quote by Avril

Harpley, who as long ago as 1990 recognised the fact that 'Media-educated children are better equipped to communicate in a variety of ways to suit a range of audiences and purposes. They have a better informed choice' (p. 5). There can surely be no doubt that exploration of the conventions of media texts helps to equip children for their future, adult world.

Summary

In this chapter we have discussed:

- the relevance of media texts in the primary classroom;

- comics and graphic books;

- promotional leaflets;

- interactive CD-ROMs;

- websites.

12

Applying text-, sentence- and word-level knowledge to digital communications

This chapter will focus on texts created by digital technologies. In recent years such texts have become 'embedded in the everyday fabric of . . . society' (Carrington and Robinson 2009: 1). Producers of these texts are able to distribute them amongst a wide range of friends, family and acquaintances and this notion impacts on our understanding of the concept of audience. A recent report in *The Guardian* newspaper (Sweney 2010) stated that a quarter of UK internet users aged between eight and 12 years had profiles on social networking sites such as Facebook and Bebo, despite the minimum age for registration being set at age thirteen. This means that primary-aged children can now be considered as 'motivated producers and consumers of digital texts' (Dowdall 2009a: 50).

This chapter will consider three forms of digital communication technology and the skills and knowledge needed to make sense of them. The text types covered will include:

- text messaging;
- virtual worlds;
- social networking.

In each case we will discuss the type of text, how the text is constructed, the choice of words and the multimodal aspects of the text (images, symbols and sounds). 'Virtual worlds' and 'social networking' relate to specific websites. In each case, selected pages will be considered as texts in their own right. Where possible, we will make comparisons with conventional written texts.

Text messages

As more people, including children, have acquired mobile phones, text messaging has become an increasingly popular form of communication. It is essentially a form of note writing that uses as few characters and spaces as possible. This ensures that the message meets its purpose of being 'speedier and less expensive' (O'Mara 2001) whilst also fulfilling its primary aim of communicating. This communicating requires both the sender and receiver to understand the conventions of text messaging. The brevity of the text message makes it an incredibly attractive form of communication for the reluctant writer. Children are increasingly using abbreviations based on a phonic system that would be acceptable in a text message in more formal styles of writing. A good example is the child who insists on writing 'u' instead of 'you'. This of course highlights the importance of using text messages as a teaching tool in order to make children aware of their purpose and to discourage such abbreviated language in more formal writing. There are three main features of text messages:

- abbreviations using phonic spellings;
- acronyms;
- emotions represented by symbols.

A typical text message

'HavAGr8DALOL' is how the sender of a text message might typically say: 'Have a great day! Laugh out loud!'

What kind of text is this?

This particular 'stand-alone' message is a note sending good wishes. Before text messaging became the preferred method of communication, such a statement would have formed part of a telephone conversation in which two parties had been discussing what they were going to do in the day ahead. The statement would probably have featured towards the end of the conversation, almost as a sign off. Therefore this message could suggest that the sender is in regular communication with the receiver and knows what is going on in their life.

Text construction and choice of words

The language is informal and formulaic in that it is made up of two turns of phrase. It is written using the imperative form of the verb, 'hav', therefore instructing the receiver to 'Have a great day' regardless of what may happen! There is no sentence punctuation as such, but there are examples of lower and upper case letters. Lower case letters represent consonants and short vowel sounds in the middle of words. Capitalisation, on the other hand, has three specific roles in text messaging, two of which are demonstrated in the message:

- to represent the start of a new word, for example 'have';
- to denote a long vowel sound in the middle of a word, for example the 'A' in 'DA' representing 'day'.

The third role is to represent a double letter as in 'happy', which would read 'HaPE'. Other ways that double letters are represented are a $ for 'ss' and a % sign for 'bb'. Numbers are also used frequently in text messaging, often for their phonic qualities. In this case the '8' represents the /eat/ sound in 'great' but uses only one character instead of three.

Acronyms

The range of acronyms used in text messaging is constantly evolving. Some of the familiar, such as 'TTFN' (ta ta for now), remain but there are many interesting newcomers such as 'KIT' (keep in touch), TBH (to be honest) and 'LOL' (laugh out loud), as shown in the example above. In the example, LOL is used as a sign off; however, it can also be used in its literal sense following an amusing remark in a text message. What is interesting is that some of these acronyms, such as LOL, are now being used in everyday speech, often as exclamations. Also, predictive text modes on mobile phones recognize them as words in their own right. In predictive text mode, the phone draws on a bank of words stored in a dictionary known as 'T9'. The keys 5, 6 and 5 are used to write 'LOL'. This appears as 'KM' until the final '5' key is pressed and the letter combination becomes 'LOL'. The phone draws on the first word with this possible combination of letters. Phone users can personalize their T9 dictionary to include less common words, colloquialisms, acronyms or proper nouns. One teenage boy included the surname of the manager of the Premiership football team he supports, as he was always sending texts to friends complaining about the manager's tactics!

Symbols and icons

Symbols are often used to express emotions. Most telephone technologies provide options to use symbols and icons via an 'Add Symbols' option but older phones will require the sender to use the punctuation options to create a symbol. For example, as previously illustrated, 'happy' can be written as 'HaPE' but could alternatively be written as ': –)'. This is a colon, followed by a dash, followed by a closing bracket. Equally it can be represented by the icon J. Some other examples are:

- ': – &' – I feel tongue tied;
- ': – @' – I am angry/screaming;
- 'L:–)' – Congratulations on your graduation!

Obviously, the aim is for the symbol to give a pictorial representation of the message.

It is clearly apparent that both sender and receiver need to be equally aware of text messaging conventions to read and make sense of any communication. Many of us still have great difficulty with text messaging and struggle not to write full words and not to punctuate! For the reluctant or uninitiated, a variety of books are available to offer instruction on text messaging. They help to clarify issues, especially those relating to acronyms and emoticons. After all, writing and interpreting text messages is 'the stuff of the Bletchley Park codebreakers' (Rifkind 2004). Good luck!

Virtual worlds

The website 'Moshi Monsters', launched in 2008, is an online virtual world and social networking site aimed at seven to 11 year olds (although it does have a much broader appeal and has users as young as three!). In March 2010 the number of registered users exceeded fifteen million, one-third of whom are UK based. Users visiting the site register to adopt a monster from one of six basic designs. They then customise its appearance and name it. The aim of the game is to keep the monster happy and healthy. Therefore, monsters must be regularly fed, and can interact with others in the virtual town created by the site (subscription members get access to more areas of the game). Educational games can be played in short sixty-second bursts and are proving to be popular with teachers for use in the primary classroom. Successful completion of the games will earn the monster Rox, the currency of the virtual world. Rox can be spent in the virtual marketplace to buy food or goods to customise the monster's living space, for example lamps and rugs. Once registered, and invited by a friend, users can leave notes on their friends' message boards. Details of friends are recorded on a friendship tree in the virtual living quarters.

This website is produced by commercial web designers who make decisions about layout and content. The homepage is simple in design, uncluttered and easy to read, with an easy-to-access toolbar and option listing. Within the site, registered users also create texts and make decisions about layout and content! Therefore it is important to consider both parties and the type of texts they produce. To do this we will focus on two main pages within the website: 'Main Street' and the 'Virtual Pinboard'. The pages will be considered as texts in their own right.

Shopping in the Main Street and Sludge Street

What kind of text is this?

This is an image-based street map of the shopping area in this virtual world. Moving the cursor around the screen enables the user to navigate and become familiar with the street network (Figure 12.1). Clicking on a shop enables the user to go inside to browse and to buy. There are moving images of other monsters going about their business and this gives a more realistic feel and purpose to the page. The only writing used takes the form of labels to name streets and shops, and general single word instructions. Longer descriptions of specific items are found when the user enters a shop.

Text construction and choice of words

The shop names all have a monster or horror connection and are examples of puns. For example, furnishings are bought at 'Yukea' (play on Ikea), and for those members who subscribe there is access to the exclusive 'Horrods' store! These examples can also be seen as being intertextual references to advertising texts and, although immediately identifiable to adults, they will be less obvious to children. Equally, it is users familiar with London who will immediately make the connection with 'Harrods', but the

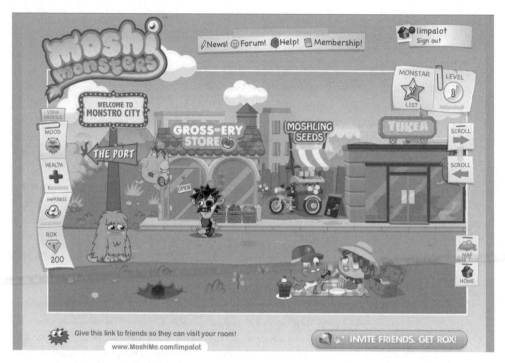

FIGURE 12.1 Moshi Monsters © Mind Candy Ltd.

significance of its exclusivity within the virtual world will not be understood if its place in the real world isn't recognised. Food is bought at the 'Gross-ery Store'. In this case 'Gross' takes on the more modern definition of 'disgusting' or 'vulgar'. This will be picked up on immediately by children and in this example it is the adults who may fail to interpret the significance of the name, as they draw on other definitions of gross, for example 'total' as in 'gross income'. This is an example of language evolving over time.

In the stores you can move the cursor over the items for sale to obtain more information. The information appears as short descriptive phrases that are demarcated like sentences. For example, in the DIY shop the shelving is described as 'Woohoo awesome shelving!' The 'Woohoo' is a ghostly play on 'ooh' and, combined with the exclamation mark at the end of the phrase, suggests that people will make positive exclamations if they see this shelving in your home. 'Awesome' is a modern, informal alternative to 'stunning', suggesting that this is an up-to-the-minute, must-have piece of furniture!

Icons, images and sounds

There are a number of icons; however, not all are clear in what they represent. The 'Red Cross' is universally symbolic of health and is appropriate but the 'Diamond' and '200' to represent the currency or 'Rox' are less obvious and require the user to have a knowledge of the slang term for diamond, 'rock', and to equate this to being of value.

The images contradict the horror connotations of the text in that they represent pastoral images of monsters picnicking or strolling down the street. The use of green as the main colour reinforces this. This suggests that it is a pleasant and safe place to be.

There are a number of accompanying sounds, for example birds singing and monsters whistling and talking in nonsense monster language! The monster speak is supported by a speech bubble that translates what the monster is saying, for example 'Grrr OOO', 'Oh it's you again!' More information about speech bubbles can be found in Chapter 11.

Virtual Pinboard

What kind of text is this?

This page is effectively an online address and notebook. Messages are written on an electronic 'Post-It' note and, as such, this puts a constraint on how much can be written at any one time. Users are encouraged to select a colour for their 'Post-It' note from sixteen colour options, the majority of which are variations of either blue or pink. There is also a selection of icons available for inclusion in the message. Colour and icons will be discussed in more detail in the 'Icons and Images' section. As the purpose of this page is for the user to communicate, we will draw on an example in which two ten-year-old girls communicate with each other. The text produced is in the form of a greeting in order to initiate a conversation.

Text construction and choice of words

The initial posting was 'Hi wuu2', meaning 'Hi, what are you up to?' There are similarities with text messaging as there is a mix of alpha/numeric characters, with words such as 'you' being represented by the letter 'u' and 'to' by the numeral '2'. Although a capital letter 'H' is used at the start of the sentence, there is no punctuation at the end of the question. Unlike text messaging, there are no further capital letters to indicate a new word. Interestingly this child does not have access to a mobile phone, yet was quite comfortable in her use of text messaging-style language. Her parents were concerned that she wasn't 'writing properly', a view supported by the Queen's English Society who are hoping to set up an English Academy to 'protect English from the spell of txt spk' (Woodcock 2010: 11). Her parents were also intrigued as to how she had learned to communicate in such a way. The child's response to how she knew what to write was, 'We just do!' The use of 'we' suggests a 'them and us' situation in which the children are in full control of how they communicate. This example also highlights the difference in attitude of the different generations towards what constitutes writing.

The immediate response from her friend was 'Can't talk now I've got to hav my tea'. This is a very different language structure. It is informal and close to speech but it is more consistent with standard alphabetic writing codes. The pronoun 'I' is omitted at the beginning of the sentence providing an example of ellipsis. The sentence has no punctuation at the end and could indeed be considered to be two sentences, as a full stop could be placed after 'now'. 'Have' is abbreviated to 'hav' but this is the only example of a phonetic spelling.

The sharp contrast in the two postings suggests that any style of writing is acceptable. However an understanding of abbreviated language forms is essential to read and understand messages. This understanding appears to come about through practice. As one teenager commented, 'You learn about text speak and acronyms by using it/them. If you don't understand what something means, you ask the sender. If you like it you use it again yourself.'

Icons and images

The 'Pinboard' page is exactly that. It is an image of a cork pinboard that will be familiar to most children, through home or school, as an accessible way of pinning up messages. The ability to change the note colour is interesting. As we have previously said, the majority of options are variations of pink and blue; in fact twelve of the sixteen options fall into this category. The child who initiated the conversation in the example above chose to use a lilac colour, the favourite colour of both her and her friend. When asked if she would send a lilac note to a boy she was horrified and said, 'No I would use blue of course!' This shows an understanding of colour as a semiotic mode, an awareness that, in her culture, blue signifies a boy. As with words, colours can denote an object (see Chapter 8). Her friend replied using the more conventional yellow note, which mirrors her approach to writing.

Neither child supported their written text with an icon as, in this example, speed was of the essence. However, the range of icons provided on the web page is extensive. It includes the emoticons found in the 'Add Symbols' option on a mobile phone (see section on 'Text Messaging') but also has a number of additions including a planet, dinosaur, football, musical notes and a Christmas cracker. The range will appeal to both girls and boys, as well as providing an icon for every occasion!

The font style is informal and childlike, similar to Comic Sans, making it appealing to the target age group.

Social networking

The 'Moshi Monsters' website has been referred to in the press as 'Facebook's little brother'. Therefore the natural progression is for us to focus on 'Facebook', the most popular social networking website across all ages. 'Facebook' allows its members to communicate with friends through writing and visual images. As with 'Moshi Monsters', users have to register. This process asks for personal information (some optional) and requires the user to have an e-mail account. The implications of this, in terms of page content and layout, will be discussed later. We will focus on two pages, referred to as texts: 'News Feed' and 'Profile'.

News Feed

What kind of text is this?

This page is essentially a comments page, although, as part of the home area, it does have other functions. It consists of a series of brief statements made by friends. This page tends to be scanned by the user, to see if there is anything of interest being posted. If there is, there is an opportunity to respond to each of the comments by clicking on the word 'comment' beneath each entry and posting a personal response, connected or otherwise. In Figure 12.2, most of the comments relate to the Eurovision Song Contest.

Layout, text construction and choice of words

The layout of this page is similar to that of the BBC website (see Chapter 11). The text on this page is constructed by a large number of individuals and, as a result, offers examples of a range of writing styles. We can begin by examining the text of the web designer. In this case it is limited to the 'option' list (found on the left-hand side of the page) and limited advertising (found on the right-hand side of the page). The second part of the options list is in alphabetical order, just like an index in a non-fiction book text. This gives a more formal structure and conventional feel to the page. There is one advert that stands out: 'Win 6 VIP tickets to the 2010 Soccer World Cup Final'. The word 'soccer' provides an example of an Americanism, as 'football' is more acceptable to an English audience.

The main body of the page is devoted to general comments made by friends. These comments take the form of a news roundup. Examining some of the inclusions from Figure 12.2 we can see examples of newspaper headline-type language in 'Not bad Cyprus'. The proper noun 'Cyprus' begins with a capital letter unlike the proper nouns in the example at the top of the page: 'german singer's english'. In the second example we do see the correct use of an apostrophe to show possession. These examples show that there isn't a total disregard for punctuation, although it is inconsistent. Each posting is a personal comment, but as each begins with the full name of the individual there is no evidence of the first person 'I' being used. This has the effect of making these personal responses rather impersonal, despite some expressing innermost thoughts, for example '. . . absolute turn on'.

Icons and images

The 'option' list is represented by an icon and an alphabetic description, for example 'Games' is represented by two playing cards with a heart and a spade on them. Users have to make the connection between 'playing' cards and the word 'games' to fully understand how the image and text work together. Also, there is an image of a mobile phone and a speech bubble informing users that they can keep in touch on their mobile phone. The choice of speech bubble is interesting, likening messages sent via 'Facebook' to a spoken conversation rather than a written message.

The font style is a clear and formal Arial style. The colour of postings is black. Blue, the official colour of Facebook, is used for instructions.

The personal images next to the users' comments are thumbnail pictures taken from their profile pictures. Selection of profile pictures will be discussed in the following section.

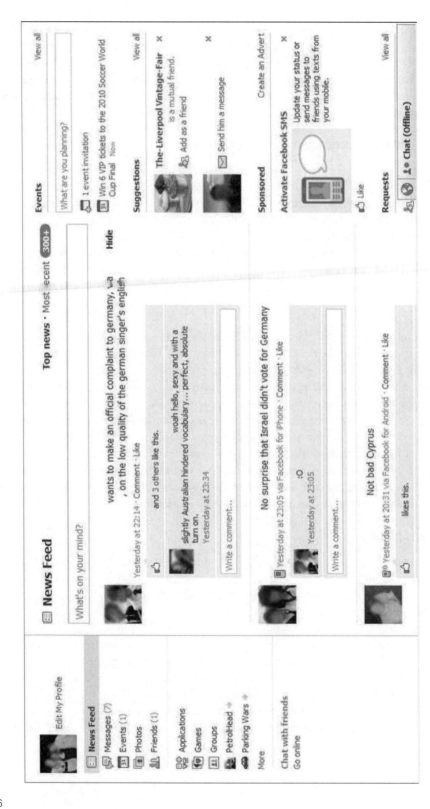

FIGURE 12.2 Example of Facebook 'News Feed' page.

The profile page

What kind of text is this?

This is perhaps the most important page in the eyes of the user as it is in this area that all personal information is kept. The user effectively creates a brief autobiography in both words and pictures. Like the previous text, it is a combination of website and user-produced communications.

Layout, text construction and choice of words

Across the top of the page is a toolbar that includes options such as 'Photos' and 'Info' (abbreviations of 'Photographs' and 'Information'). The 'Photos' area is important to the user and will be discussed later. The 'Info' area takes the form of a formal questionnaire and asks for information including interests. The website can access this information to ensure that advertising is targeted towards the user's personal interests. For example, one teenage boy who has interests including football, cricket and rock climbing had a large advert posted for 'Twenty20' cricket tickets. Although this is an example of irrelevant information that can be ignored, the fact that it is of personal interest will make it more likely that the user will read and take notice of it.

The profile picture, to be discussed in the next section, is accompanied by the user's 'status'. This is a comment relating to how he or she is feeling, or what they have been doing. An example from a male teenager taking public exams is: 'x is really stressed! Glad when exams over!' The status is updated regularly. Users are not embarrassed to share their feelings with others. There is nothing private about social networking!

To start a conversation the user clicks on the 'chat' option and selects the friend with whom they want to converse. They then write a message. Messages can be read by anybody authorised to access the individual's pages. If the user wants a private conversation they have to click on the speech bubble icon at the top of the page. We can now look at an extract from a conversation that began by asking how the individual was keeping. The response was:

> I've been keeping well ta :) I'm a little upset about not having gone to Akro, but hey ho : p.

We can see that this comment is very close to spoken language. There are examples of contractions: 'I've' and 'I'm' instead of 'I have' and 'I am'. We have colloquialisms, for example 'ta' instead of the standard English 'thank you', and an abbreviation of Akrotiri (Cyprus), 'Akro'. There are also symbols to represent mood. The first is a smiley face, ':)', suggesting happiness and the second, ': p', which represents an individual sticking out their tongue, suggests an altogether different emotion of resignation. Users adapt these symbols to suit their needs. For example, if feeling very happy an additional mouth may be added, ':))', or some will add a nose: ': o)'. Personalisation, within an understood framework, is the order of the day!

Icons, images and sound

The user 'profile' picture is the dominant image on the page. The user can change the picture at any time by moving the curser over the picture and clicking on 'change picture'. Users generally select their profile picture carefully, as they realise it tells their circle of friends a lot about them. As one teenager said, 'You want it to portray you positively'. What constitutes a positive image will of course depend upon the circle of friends and their interests. It is when selecting their image that users are most aware of their audience.

There are a number of icons shown on this page. In fact, each option is represented by both icon and text; for example 'album' is represented by a silhouette in a frame. Colours are restricted to icons and images and the blue font for instructions and web links.

Users are able to select and include their favourite music or sketches. They do this by creating weblinks to sites such as 'YouTube'. Like the profile picture, the choice of music is carefully considered as it works alongside the text and photograph to create an image of the user. Music, like the photographs, is selected to appeal to peers. Audio modes are accompanied by a posting, for example 'Quality tune plus link'. The focus is on the music link, not the written word, therefore writing is kept to a minimum. The word 'quality' suggests that the user holds the piece in high regard. Nothing else needs to be said. The choice of the noun 'tune' is interesting as to older generations it appears to be old-fashioned and feels rather anachronistic. However, as a number of teenagers agreed, 'Its not old-fashioned, it is a word we use all of the time, think of "iTunes" '. 'Apple' and its range of technologies have brought this noun back into fashion!

Audience

In Chapter 4 we commented about how texts are created with an audience in mind and throughout this chapter we have touched on the concept of audience. Digital communications do offer the potential to communicate with a wide range of people and as such the concept of audience can be blurred. We have seen that when communicating on 'Facebook' the individual is very aware of audience when selecting visual and audio representations. They are manufactured elements of the communication process. In fact, more responsible users ask friends for permission before using a photograph. However, in all of the above digital communications, less thought is given to the audience of the written text. Perhaps this is because the idea of friendship has been extended to include anybody who is known to the individual, and friends are addressed in a more informal register. This can be a problem when formal messages have to be written. Some primary schools and universities are asking students to use standard English when communicating with staff through e-mail or using virtual learning platforms.

In this chapter we have considered a variety of texts created using digital technologies. In all cases these texts, although written, are very close to speech in their construction. They offer the text producer the opportunity to integrate visual and audio modes in the text construction. As teachers it is important that we not only understand how language is constructed but also recognise children's intentions and the sources of their influences when they create these texts (McClay 2002: 47).

Summary

In this chapter we have discussed:

- the relevance of digital communications to primary-aged children;

- text messaging;

- virtual worlds;

- social networking;

- audience and digital communications.

13

Conclusion

It will have become apparent if you have read the book thus far that in describing language knowledge, whether at text, sentence or word level, we have been at pains to include both speaking and writing. They are not identical at any of these three levels, although there are large areas of overlap. Ron Carter (1994) claims that understanding the differences between speech and writing is one of the most important aspects of language knowledge for teachers, and we agree with this. The Rose review (Rose 2006), amongst other recent government publications, has made it clear that the development of speech and writing are of equal importance.

It is not easy for schools as social institutions to provide opportunities for pupils to participate in the full range of speech situations they will meet in life. Drama can go some way towards extending the range, but even here there are limitations. There are two types of speaking and listening, however, that schools are ideally set up to provide opportunities for. One is talking to learn: to identify a question or an issue; to explore it; to share ideas with others; to reflect on what has been learned and to think about how one can apply the learning, all the time building up one's confidence in oneself as a learner. The second is talking to build and maintain the life of the community, in this case the school. This includes learning to explore aspects of one's own and others' behaviour; to make decisions with others; and to negotiate over rules and practices.

Speaking and listening is so much a part of everyday life, of the way we negotiate our relationships, our jobs, our hobbies and interests, and above all our sense of ourselves and our place in the world, that schools must ensure they give it as much care and attention as they do literacy.

This brings us to the second point we want to emphasise in this concluding chapter: that the roots of the language are in everyday speech. Steven Pinker (2003: 7) makes the point well when he says:

> There is a world of elegance and richness in quotidian speech that far outshines the local curiosities of etymologies, unusual words and fine points of usage.

This respect for the significance of the language we all use to carry out our daily lives is at the heart of what we think is important in developing language knowledge. In 1964, Alec Clegg, in *The Excitement of Writing*, wrote:

A *minority* of pupils in the schools of this country are born into families whose members speak *the normal language* of educated society . . . There are, however, other children, *possibly a majority in industrial areas*, who have to learn this *acceptable* language at school but who, in some cases, may well face discouragement, or even derision, if they venture to use it at home.

(p. 1, our italics)

Nowadays, we find this way of thinking unacceptable. It seems to us that any society that is prepared to write off the language of the majority of its citizens as 'abnormal' or 'unacceptable' is in a very perilous state. This is not for one moment to deny that there is such a thing as slovenly or incorrect speech and writing produced in any dialect, standard or non-standard.

We start out, each one of us, by learning the spoken language of our home and of our community. These, to return to our metaphor, are our language roots. If we could develop the metaphor briefly, we are very fortunate that the 'tree' of the English language, developed and enriched over hundreds of years, has very many branches. Some of them are a great way off the ground, but they are accessible to those who are prepared to scramble up. If some children get stuck or fall off in doing so, our job is not to tell them off and bring them back to safety, but to give them better scrambling skills.

To acquire more knowledge about the construction of texts, the structure of sentences, the choice of words, is to be empowered as a speaker, listener, reader or writer. The empowerment of our pupils must be an important aim of all our teaching, or it is worth nothing, regardless of statistics that show improved test results. Teachers can pass on knowledge about these language systems, and make them interesting and exciting to children, only if they are secure in them themselves. That must come first. What follows is very, very much more difficult: to find the right ways to pass the knowledge on to pupils. This has been a book about the first phase: the development of teachers' own language knowledge. We would like to end with some thoughts about how the pupils might benefit in the next stage, because that, in the end, is what really matters.

A learner by taking part in rule-governed social behaviour may pick up the rules by means hardly distinguishable from the processes by which they were first socially derived – and by which they continue to be amended. On the other hand, along may come the traditional teacher and, with the best intentions, trying to be helpful, set out to observe the behaviour, analyse to codify the rules and teach the outcome as a recipe. Yes, this may sometimes be helpful, but as a consistent pedagogy it is manifestly counterproductive . . . We have a choice: we can operate so as to make [the classroom] as rich an interactive learning community as we can, or we may continue to treat it as a captive audience for whatever instruction we choose to offer.

(Britton 1994: 263)

Commentaries

Activity 1: The primary teaching context

(a)   Home/school contrasts: you might like to compare your ideas with what is said in Chapter 3 of this book.

(b)   Speech/writing contrasts: see pages 30–1 and 54–5.

(c)   See Chapters 4 and 5 for discussion of what we know about texts. Chapters 6 and 7 explore aspects of grammatical knowledge; Chapter 8 looks at word-level knowledge.

(d)   Chapters 4–8 contain some of the terminology we can use to share and extend implicit knowledge. However, please remember our warning that the teaching of terminology is not the most important aspect of your work. Pupils parroting terms they only half understand would be a retrograde step in their language development. Above all, as a teacher you must try to devise what Helen Bromley (2000: 2) calls 'shared contexts for the joint creation of fresh understandings'. She has some helpful suggestions to make on how this can be done. You must think very hard about the part some language terminology shared by pupils and teachers might play in building these contexts.

Activity 2: Text-level work

1(a)   'Purpose' is a key concept in discussing texts but a tricky one. An author can have many purposes for writing a single text: to inform, to amuse, to excite, to curry favour with someone – to make money, even! Here we are only concerned with the function or purpose of the words themselves, and not any underlying considerations.

■   The extract suggests that the text was primarily designed to inform its readers – to give them information about dinosaurs. This would put it, in National Curriculum terms, into the category of 'report' texts. For more information, see pages 36–7.

■   The title of the text provides the first clue as to the type of text it will be. There are also clues in the illustrations on the front cover, and in the blurb on the back. Children need to develop their skills in selecting texts that will be appropriate for their purposes and should have their attention drawn to these features from a very early age. In approaching both fiction and non-fiction texts they should learn to look for the names of authors, publishers and series they have met before and found enjoyable.

1(b) There is evidence to suggest that the book was written for young readers. This includes:

- the grammatical form chosen for the opening sentence;

- the direct address to the reader in several of the sentences;

- the exhortation to imagine what it was like to be alive at the time, using the senses as a way in;

- the use of some informal vocabulary such as 'munching mouths';

- the amount of detail the writer includes: enough to interest and inform, but not as much as an adult or specialist reader would require. 'Scientists who studied . . .' is an example. A specialist reader would not be content with this degree of vagueness but would expect chapter and verse on which scientists and when.

1(c) There seems to be a change in the structure of the text when the author gets to 'Dinosaurs lived millions of years ago . . .'

1(d) In general terms, the first part of the text seems to be directly addressed to the readers, urging them to imagine what it would have been like to live at the time of the dinosaurs. The second part switches to providing the readers with facts and figures about dinosaurs.

1(e) If you have seen this as an informative text, rather than, say, a story about dinosaurs, you will probably be expecting more about such things as:

- what types of dinosaur there were;

- what they ate;

- how and where they made their homes;

- why they became extinct.

All these points are covered in the book. It is an important part of the teaching of reading from Key Stage 1 onwards to encourage children to go to texts with clear expectations of what they will find in them. Sometimes it's helpful to get children to formulate some questions before they start to read the text.

1(f) We access many non-fiction texts differently from the way we read stories and poems, not always starting at the beginning and reading through to the end. In locating the bits of information we want, we find the following helpful:

- contents pages;

- headings and subheadings in bold type;

- information in boxes, sometimes with a different coloured background from the rest of the page;

- indexes;

■ diagrams, pictures and so on, which stand out clearly from the pieces of written text.

Inevitably, some of the vocabulary used will be quite specialised. Glossaries are useful in explaining technical terms. An introduction to all of the above also forms part of reading instruction from the Early Years.

2(a) This is from a text giving instructions on how to make a puppet. The verb in the imperative would be a strong clue here; instructional texts are telling us to do something.

2(b) This is part of an explanation of how chocolate is made.

2(c) This might have been a personal recount; we can hear the voice of the speaker coming through strongly, telling us his story. In fact, it is from a novel, *Isaac Campion*, by Janni Howker (2003), written in the first person.

2(d) This is from a child's piece of writing, persuading us to consider an issue from her point of view.

2(e) This is the opening two lines of the poem 'The Highwayman' by Alfred Noyes (Noyes and Keeping 1983). Rhyme, rhythm and figurative language combine to make this extract easy to recognise.

2(f) This is another piece written by a child, recounting what happened on a school trip.

If you were able to recognise these short extracts it was because as an adult you have come across texts like these before – you 'know how they go'. For a more detailed look at some of the syntactic and lexical choices that might have prompted your decision, see the activities following Chapters 6 and 7, and Chapter 8.

Activity 3: Sentence-level work

1(a) A question. It's a good idea to use this type of sentence as the opening of a factual text for young readers. It may engage their attention and stimulate some imaginative involvement.

1(b) A statement.

1(c) An instruction.

1(d) An exclamation.

2(a) Complex.

2(b) Compound.

2(c) Simple.

2(d) Simple.

This is an area of grammar that many people claim to find difficult to discuss explicitly, although all of us use a variety of these sentence structures quite spontaneously from a very young age. See Chapter 7 for more information.

3(a)   One way of dividing the passage into chunks would be as follows:

Imagine/the sight and smell/of a herd/of 40-tonne Brachiosaurus/in a conifer forest,/pine needles showering down/from their munching mouths,/14 metres above you.

3(b)   To some extent the position and the number of commas is a matter of the writer's judgement. A colleague who sometimes used to act as a response partner for us tells us that we use far too many! You might have felt that you wanted to add a comma after 'Brachiosaurus' but omit the one after 'munching mouths'.

3(c)   In the second reconstructed sentence, 'Recent discoveries have shattered this view, we now know that dinosaurs were a great success', the comma is not as satisfactory as the full stop. Some reasons for this are as follows:

■   Each part, before and after the comma, constitutes a clause in its own right, because each has its own subject and a verb.

■   It's true that the ideas in the two clauses are related but each idea has been expressed in a way that makes it syntactically independent. The two parts are of equal weight; neither is 'subordinate' to the other. We have two main clauses here.

■   The two clauses could have been linked by a coordinating conjunction such as 'and': 'Recent discoveries have shattered this view and we now know that dinosaurs were a great success.'

■   Writers have important decisions to make about whether to let their sentences stand alone, or to make them flow into each other. The use of conjunctions such as 'and' is only one way of joining parts of a text together. This area will be an important part of the work on writing you do with children. See pages 77–9 if you would like to find out more.

■   If the second clause is allowed to stand alone, after a fairly substantial pause provided by a full stop, it provides a more dramatic conclusion to the whole of the second part of the text, enticing the reader to go on and find out more.

You should ensure that you are confident about the use of other types of punctuation such as apostrophes, question marks and speech marks. The teaching of punctuation will be an important part of your work with children. Trainees on IT courses in England are required to pass tests to ascertain their level of skills in punctuation, as well as spelling, comprehension and grammar. If you would like to know more about punctuation you can find help by using the index of this book. A particularly useful publication is that by Challen (2001).

4   Passive. The cocoa beans are having something done to them by someone (not specified). The purpose of this text, as we have seen, is to explain the chocolate-making process. Cocoa beans are central to this, and presumably the writer wants to keep our attention firmly focused on them and not on the people engaged in carrying out the process. Using the passive enables the writer to

keep 'cocoa beans' as the subject of the sentences. (See pages 55–8 and 67–8 if you would like to find out more about the construction of sentences.)

5(a) Make [sentence (c)] or let [sentence (d)].

5(b) To have lived [sentence (a)] or to go [sentence (b)]. (For more information, see pages 62–8).

6(a) In this sentence 'book' refers to an object you can see, touch and feel. It's acting as a noun.

6(b) The word can also refer to an action, as in 'I book my theatre tickets through an agent.' In a phrase such as 'bookshelf' or 'bookshop' the word is behaving as an adjective, giving more information about a noun ('shelf' and 'shop' respectively).

If you would like to find out more about word classes you can find information on pages 58–68 and by using the index of this book.

7(a) The term 'standard English' refers to 'that variety of English which is usually used in print and which is normally taught in schools and to non-native speakers using the language' (LINC 1992: 355). For more information, see pages 50–4.

7(b) Accent refers to the ways in which speakers pronounce the sounds of English. Dialect refers to varieties of grammar and vocabulary.

7(c) There are no examples of non-standard grammar in this passage. (An example would have been if the writer had said 'I were twelve', in which a single subject is sometimes followed, in some regional dialects, by a plural verb.) Some of the vocabulary, however, would not be used in the same way in a standard English text. Examples are:

- 'Now then' as a sentence opening;
- 'rising' thirteen;
- 'our' Daniel;
- 'aye';
- 'a time of day eighty-three years back'.

Activity 4: Word-level work

1 Among the points you might have chosen are the following:

- The trees are personified – they have 'fingers' that crack in the icy wind.
- 'Crack' is an onomatopoeic word; that is, it conjures up the sound of the action it describes. This 'sound effect' is reinforced by having 'black', a word with the same sound (an internal rhyme), in the previous line.
- There's an effective comparison of the cattle with boulders, standing stock still in the icy fields (this is an example of a simile).

■ The breath of the cattle is vividly described as hanging 'in rags' (a metaphor).

We hope this small taste might have encouraged you to want to read the whole poem. You can find it, and a discussion of it, on p. x. If you want to pursue the topic of figurative language (personification, similes and metaphors) you will find the index helpful.

2   According to *Words Borrowed From Other Languages* by Sue Palmer and Eugenia Low (1998), a large-format book ideal for Key Stage 2, the origins of the words are as follows:

(a)   chocolate: from the Aztec word 'xococatl' meaning 'bitter weather';

(b)   tattoo: from a Tahitian word 'tatau' meaning 'mark';

(c)   hubbub: from the Irish Gaelic 'hooboobbes,' a cry of victory;

(d)   lady: from the Old English 'hlaefdige' meaning 'a kneader of bread'.

You can find more comments on the excitement of words in Chapter 8.

3(a)   Segmenting words into phonemes or individual sounds is one of the most difficult of the 'splitting activities'. It's surprising how many adults can't do it easily, and for dyslexics it's extremely difficult. There are four sounds in 'bread' (b/r/e/d); 'b' and 'r' are known as a 'consonant cluster'. When the word is spoken, they come out very closely aligned, though they can each be distinguished if you listen very carefully. The 'e' and the 'a', on the other hand, cannot be heard as separate sounds. They work as one to make the 'e' sound you hear. This type of spelling, in which two letters of the alphabet represent one vowel sound, is known as a vowel digraph. For more information, see page 95.

3(b)   In this group, you probably noticed this pattern:

■ br ead;

■ h ead;

■ l ead;

■ d ead.

This is a family of words with the same 'rime' (the part of the word or syllable that contains the vowel and the final consonant or consonant cluster). The part of the word before the vowel ('br', 'h', 'l', 'd') is known as the onset. In a case like this, if children can gain instant recognition of this 'rime family' it will be of more help to them than splitting the words into individual sounds.

3(c)   A morpheme is the smallest unit of meaning in a word. All of these words share one morpheme, 'lead', but others have been added to give a variety of meanings. The morphemes 'er', 'ing' and 's' are suffixes, because they have been added to the end of the word, and they change its grammatical function in each case. The morpheme 'mis' is a prefix because it goes at the front of the word and changes its meaning. Examples of prefixes and suffixes will crop up again and again in children's reading, and familiarity with them will also help their spelling if they learn to recognise them as groups of language features. For more on morphemes, see pages 88–9.

3(d)   One-syllable names include Ann, Jane, Tom, Ben. Those with two syllables include Peter, Charlie, Susan, Helen. Some three-syllable names are Amanda, Christopher, Jennifer, Rhiannon. Again, this splitting into syllables is a useful reading skill. Reading the names of animals such as 'giraffe' and 'monkey' is best tackled this way, at least as an initial strategy.

4   You might have come up with 'e' as in 'cedar', or 'ey' as in 'keys', or 'ee' as in 'meet' or 'ei' as in 'ceiling' or 'ie' as in 'field'. English spelling is quite challenging for many children (and students!). Remembering the following points might help:

- Some spellings are governed by grammatical rules [as in the suffixes we looked at in (c) above]. A good example is the past tense of regular verbs, which is always spelt '-ed' (though these don't all sound the same – compare 'wanted' and 'spoiled' and 'cropped').

- Understanding a prefix such as 'tele' or 'psych' will open the door to spelling and understanding a whole family of words such as 'psychiatrist' and 'psychology' and 'psychometric'.

- There are some spelling rules that, by continuous repetition, can help with such words as 'field' and 'ceiling' above.

Bibliography

ACCAC (2000) *English in the National Curriculum in Wales*. Cardiff: HMSO.

Alexander, R. (2008) *Towards Dialogic Teaching* (4th edition). York: Dialogos.

Baldwin, P. (2008) *The Primary Drama Handbook: An Introduction*. London: Sage.

Baldwin, P. and Flemming, K. (2002) *Teaching Literacy through Drama: Creative Approaches*. Oxon: Routledge.

Brice-Heath, S. (1983) *Ways With Words: Language, Life and Work in Communities and Classrooms*. Cambridge. Cambridge University Press.

British Film Institute (n.d.) Education resources, www.bfi.org.uk.

Britton, J. (1970) *Language and Learning*. London: Allen Lane.

Britton, J. (1994) 'Vygotsky's contribution to pedagogical theory', in S. Brindley (ed.) *Teaching English*. London: Routledge.

Bromley, H. (2000) *Book-Based Reading Games*. London: CLPE.

Bruner, J. (1983) *Child's Talk*. New York: Norton.

Byatt, A.S. (1985) *Still Life*. London: Chatto and Windus.

Byrne, J. (2003) *Create Your Own Cartoons*. London: Puffin.

Carrington, V. and Robinson, M. (eds) (2009) *Digital Literacies: Social Learning and Classroom Practices*. London: UKLA.

Carter, R. (1991) 'The new grammar teaching', in R. Carter (ed.) *Knowledge About Language and the Curriculum*. London: Hodder Arnold.

Carter, R. (1994) 'Standard Englishes in teaching and learning', in M. Hayhoe and S. Parker (eds) *Who Owns English?* Buckingham: Open University Press.

Challen, D. (2001) *Primary English: Audit and Test: Assessing your Knowledge and Understanding*. Exeter: Learning Matters.

Clegg, A.B. (ed.) (1964) *The Excitement of Writing*. London: Chatto and Windus.

Clipson Boyles, S. (1998) *Drama in Primary English Teaching*. London: David Fulton Publishers.

Collins Gem (1997) *Spelling Guide*. London: HarperCollins Publishers.

Cousins, J. (1999) *Listening to Four Year Olds*. London: The National Early Years Network.

Craggs, C. (1992) *Media Education in the Primary School*. London: Routledge.

Crystal, D. (1987) *The Cambridge Encyclopedia of Language*. Cambridge: Cambridge University Press.

Crystal, D. (2004a) *Rediscover Grammar*. Harlow: Longman.

Crystal, D. (2004b) *Making Sense of Grammar*. Harlow: Longman.

de Bernières, L. (1994) *Captain Corelli's Mandolin*. London: Secker and Warburg.

DCSF (2005) No longer available in print. Available at http://nationalstrategies.standards.dcsf.gov.uk/strands.34758/34268/110206 (accessed 21 October 2010).

DCSF (2008) *Statutory Framework for the Early Years Foundation Stage*. Nottingham: DCSF.

DES (1978) *Primary Education in England*. London: HMSO.

DfEE (1998) *The National Literacy Strategy*. London: DfEE.

DfEE/QCA (1999) *The National Curriculum. Handbook for Primary Teachers in England*. London: HMSO.

DfES (2003) *Excellence and Enjoyment. A Strategy for Primary Schools*. London: HMSO.

DfES/QCA (2003) *Speaking, Listening and Learning: Working with Children in Key Stages 1 and 2*. London: HMSO.

DfES/QCA (2006) *Primary Framework for Literacy and Mathematics*. London: DfES.

Dowdall, C. (2009a) 'Masters and critics; children as producers of online digital texts', in Carrington, V. and Robinson, M. (eds) *Digital Literacies: Social Learning and Classroom Practices*. London: UKLA.

Dowdall, C. (2009b) 'Impressions, improvisations and compositions: reframing children's text production in social network sites', *Literacy*, 43 (2): 91–9.

Earl, L., Watson, N., Levin B., Leithwood, K., Fullan, M. and Torrance, N. with Jantzi, D., Mascall, B. and Volante, L. (2003) Watching and Learning 3: Final Report of the External Evaluation of England's National Literacy and Numeracy Strategies. Toronto: Ontario Institute for Studies in Education.

Evans, J. (2004) *Literacy Moves On: Using Popular Culture, New Technologies and Critical Literacy in the Primary Classroom*. London: David Fulton Publishers.

Foale, J. and Pagett, L. (2008) *Creative Approaches to Poetry for the Primary Framework for Literacy*. London: David Fulton Publishers.

Foster-Cohen, S.H. (1999) *An Introduction to Child Language Development*. London: Longman.

Fowler, H.W. *et al.* (eds) (1996) *Pocket Oxford Dictionary*. Oxford: Oxford University Press.

Fromkin, V., Rodman, R. and Hyams, N. (2010) *An Introduction to Language*. Boston: Heinle and Heinle.

Gamble, N. and Yates, S. (2008) *Exploring Children's Literature* (2nd edition). London: Sage.

Goodwin, P. (2001) 'Make time for storytime', *Literacy Today*, 25.

Goswami, U. and Bryant, P. (1990) *Phonological Skills and Learning to Read*. London: Psychology Press.

Halliday, M. (1973) *Explorations in the Functions of Language*. London: Edward Arnold.

Halliday, M. (1985) *An Introduction to Functional Grammar*. London: Edward Arnold.

Harpley, A. (1990) *Bright Ideas for Media Education*. Leamington Spa: Scholastic.

Holmes, J. (2008) *An Introduction to Sociolinguistics*. London: Longman.

Keith, G. and Shuttleworth, J. (2000) *Living Language: Exploring Advanced A Level English Language*. London: Hodder Arnold.

Kervin, L. (2009) 'GetReel: engaging Year 6 students in planning, scripting, actualising and evaluating media texts', *Literacy*, 43 (1), 29–35.

Kress, G. (2003) *Literacy in the New Media Age*. Oxon: Routledge.

Kress, G. (2004), 'Social semiotics and multimodal texts', in Somekh, B. and Lewin, C. (eds) *Research Methods in the Social Sciences*. London: Sage.

Lakoff, G. and Johnson, M. (2003) *Metaphors We Live By*. Chicago: University of Chicago Press.

Lehmann, R. (1936) *The Weather in the Streets*. Glasgow: William Collins.

Lewis, C.S. (1969) 'On three ways of writing for children', in S. Egof, G.T. Stubbs and L.F. Ashley (eds) *Only Connect*. Toronto: Oxford University Press.

Lewis, M. and Wray, D. (1996) *Developing Children's Non-Fiction Writing*. Leamington Spa: Scholastic.

LINC (1992) *Language in the National Curriculum: Materials for Professional Development*. Unpublished.

McArthur, T. and McArthur R. (eds) (2005) *Concise Oxford Companion to the English Language*. Oxford: Oxford University Press.

McClay, J.K. (2002) 'Hidden treasure: new genres, new media and the teaching of writing', *English in Education*, 36 (1), 46–55.

MacClure, M. and French, P. (1981) 'A comparison of talk at home and at school', in G. Wells (ed.) *Learning through Interaction. The Study of Language Development*. Cambridge: Cambridge University Press.

Mallett, M. (2003) *Early Years Non-Fiction: A Guide to Helping Young Researchers Use Information Texts*. London: Routledge Falmer.

Mallett, M. (2007) *The Primary English Encyclopedia*. London: David Fulton Publishers.

Medwell, J., Coates, L., Wray, D. and Griffiths, V. (2009) *Primary English: Teaching Theory and Practice (Achieving QTS)* (4th edition). Exeter: Learning Matters.

Meek, M. (1988) *How Texts Teach What Readers Learn*. Stroud: Thimble Press.

Meek, M. (1990) 'What do we know about reading that helps us teach?', in R. Carter (ed.) *Knowledge about Language and the Curriculum*. London: Hodder and Stoughton.

Meek, M. (1991) *On Being Literate*. London: Bodley Head.

Mercer, N. (1995) *The Guided Construction of Knowledge: Talk among Teacher and Learners*. Clevedon: Multilingual Matters.

Montgomery, M. (2008) *An Introduction to Language and Society* (2nd edition). London: Routledge.

Moss, G. (2007) *Literacy and Gender Researching Texts, Contexts and Readers*. Oxon: Routledge.

Moyles, J., Hargreaves, L., Merry, R. and Paterson, F. (2003) *Interactive Teaching in the Primary School. Digging Deeper into Meaning*. Buckingham: Open University Press.

Murray, W. (1969) *Teaching Reading*. Loughborough: Wills and Hepworth.

Oates, J. and Grayson, A. (eds) (2004) *Cognitive and Language Development in Children*. Oxford: Blackwell.

Ofsted (2003) *Strategies in Action: Case Studies of Improving and Declining Schools*. London: Ofsted.

O'Mara, M. (2001) *Litl bk ofpwr txt*. London: Michael O'Mara.

Ontario Institute for Studies in Education (2003) *Watching and Learning 3*. Toronto: University of Toronto.

Oxford Dictionaries (2008) *Compact Oxford English Dictionary of Current English*. Oxford. Oxford University Press.

Pinker, S. (2003) *The Language Instinct: The New Science of Language and Mind*. London: Allen Lane.

Pollock, J. and Waller, E. (1999) *English Grammar and Teaching Strategies: A Lifeline to Literacy*. London: David Fulton Publishers.

QCA (1999) *Early Learning Goals*. London: QCA.

QCA/DfEE (2000) *Curriculum Guidance for the Foundation Stage*. London: HMSO.

Rifkind, H. (2004) 'Sorry but the CIA is still sinister', *The Times*, 9 April, T2, p. 3.

Riley, J. (1996) *The Teaching of Reading: The Development of Literacy in the Early Years of School*. London: Paul Chapman.

Rose, J. (2006) *Independent Review of the Teaching of Early Reading*. Nottingham: DfES.

Schwab, I. (1994) 'Literacy, language variety and identity', in M. Hamilton, D. Barton and R. Ivanic (eds) *Worlds of Literacy*. Clevedon: Multilingual Matters.

Skutnabb-Kangas, T. and Cummins, J. (eds) (1988) *Minority Education: From Shame to Struggle*. Clevedon: Multilingual Matters.

Sweney, M. (2010) 'Quarter of eight-to-12-year-olds on Facebook, MySpace or Bebo', *The Guardian*, 26 March, www.guardian.co.uk.

TDA (2006) *Professional Standards for Teachers*. London: TDA.

Tizard, B. and Hughes, M. (1986) *Young Children Learning. Talking and Thinking at Home and at School*. London: Fontana.

Tomlinson, D. (1994) 'Errors in the research into the effectiveness of grammar teaching', *English in Education*, 28 (1) 20–6.

Trudgill, P., Hughes A. and Watt D. (2005) *English Accents and Dialects: An Introduction to Social and Regional Varieties of English in the British Isles* (4th edition). London: Hodder Education.

University of Newcastle (1999) *Ways Forward with ICT: Effective Pedagogy Using Information and Communications Technology in Literacy and Numeracy in Primary Schools*. London: TTA.

Vygotsky, L. (1962) *Thought and Language*. Cambridge, MA: MIT Press.

Wells, G. (1987) *The Meaning Makers: Children Learning Language and Using Language to Learn*. London: Hodder and Stoughton.

Whitehead, M. (1997) *Language and Literacy in the Early Years*. London: Paul Chapman.

Woodcock, N. (2010) 'Pedants' revolt aims to protect English from spell of txt spk', *The Times*, 7 June, p. 11.

Woolland, B. (2010) *Teaching Primary Drama*. Harlow: Pearson Education.

Wray, D. and Lewis, M. (1997) *Extending Literacy. Children Reading and Writing Non-Fiction*. London: Routledge.

Wray, D. and Medwell, J. (1998) *Teaching English in Primary Schools. A Handbook of Teaching Strategies and Key Ideas In Literacy*. London: Letts Educational.

Children's Books

Allen, N. (2000) *The Queen's Knickers*. London: Red Fox.

Beano (2004) 'Minnie the Minx,' in *Beano*, No. 3216. London: DC Thomson.

Biesty, S. and Platt, R. (2000) *Stephen Biesty's Incredible Everything*. London: Dorling Kindersley.

Bingham, C. (2009) *Dinosaur Encyclopedia* (first reference). London: Dorling Kindersley.

Briggs, R. (2001) *Ug, Boy Genius of the Stone Age*. London: Jonathan Cape.

Brown, R. (1992) *A Dark Dark Tale*. London: Anderson Press.

French, V. and Wisenfeld, A. (1996) *Spider Watching*. London: Walker Books.

Gardner, H. (ed.) (1972) *New Oxford Book of English Verse*. Oxford: Oxford University Press.

Goodhart, P. and Lambert, S. (2007) *Row Your Boat*. London: Picture Mammoth.

Grahame, K. (1983) *The Wind in the Willows*. London: Kestrel Books. First published in 1908.

Gribbin, J. and Gribbin, M. (1994) *Eyewitness Science: Time and Space*. London: Dorling Kindersley.

Harrison, M. and Stuart-Clark, C. (eds) (1996) *A Year Full of Poems*. Oxford: Oxford University Press.

Hook, J. and Hook R. (2000) *People Who Made History: Native Americans*. London: Hodder Wayland.

Horacek, P. (2008) *Look Out, Suzy Goose*. London: Walker Books.

Howker, J. (2003) *Isaac Campion*. London: Walker Books.

Hughes, T. (1971) *How the Whale Became*. London: Puffin.

Lewis, C.S. (1980) *The Lion, the Witch and the Wardrobe*. London: Collins. First published in 1950.

Manning, M. and Granström, B. (2004) *Splish, Splash, Splosh! A Book About Water*. London: Franklin Watts.

Noyes, A. and Keeping, C. (1983) *The Highwayman*. Oxford: Oxford University Press.

Palmer, S. and Low, E. (1998) *Words Borrowed from Other Languages*. Harlow: Longman.

Pitcher, C. and Morris, J. (1999) *The Time of the Lion*. London: Frances Lincoln.

Platt, R. and Riddell, C. (2003) *Pirate Diary. The Journal of Jake Carpenter*. London: Walker Books.

Rowling, J.K. (1997) *Harry Potter and the Philosopher's Stone*. London: Bloomsbury.

Sendak, M. (2000) *Where the Wild Things Are*. London: Bodley Head.

Sharratt, N. (2005) *Don't Put Your Finger in the Jelly, Nelly*. Leamington Spa: Scholastic.

Stickland, P. and Stickland, H. (2005) *Dinosaur Roar*. London: Puffin.

Theodorou, R. (1995) *When Dinosaurs Ruled the Earth*. Hove: Wayland.

Waddell, M. and Benson, P. (2006) *Owl Babies*. London: Walker Books.

Wilson, G. and Parkins, D. (1997) *Prowlpuss*. London: Walker Books.

Index